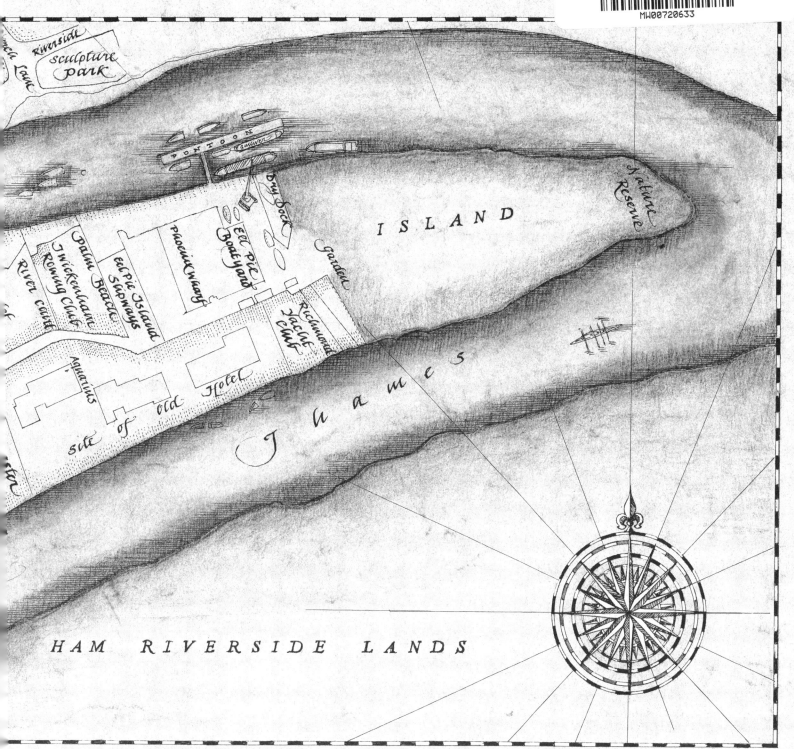

Riverside
Sculpture
Park

PONTOON

Dry Dock

Nature
Reserve

I S L A N D

Palm Beach

Twickenham
Rowing Club

River courts

Eel Pie Island
Slipways

Phoenix Wharf

Eel Pie
Boatyard

Garden

Richmond
Yacht
Club

Aquarius

site of old Hotel

T h a m e s

H A M   R I V E R S I D E   L A N D S

270 mm

300 mm

Sunrise
Jacobs Ladder
The Sycamores
Ripple
Wyndfall
Tideway
Wild Thyme
Run Softly
Desdemona
The Cottage
Kingslee
Piecrust
Copper Beech
Shamrock

Eel Pie Island

Eel Pie Island

DAN VAN DER VAT . MICHELE WHITBY

Page 1: Housing 'menu' on the side path at Eel Pie Island.

Pages 2–3: Eel Pie Island from Twickenham Embankment.

BELOW: Heron at dawn.

Frances Lincoln Limited
4 Torriano Mews
Torriano Avenue
London NW5 2RZ

Eel Pie Island
First published in the UK by Frances Lincoln Limited
in 2009
Copyright © 2009 Dan van der Vat and Michele Whitby

The authors have asserted their moral right to be
identified as Authors of this Work in accordance
with the Copyright, Designs and Patents Act 1988

Map on endpapers © 2009 Catherine Horton
Edited and designed by Jane Havell Associates

A catalogue record for this book is available from
the British Library

ISBN 978-0-7112-3053-8

Printed in Singapore

9 8 7 6 5 4 3 2

Contents

Eel Pie Island looks too small to merit a written history of its own: it is only 550 metres long and 135 at its widest. Yet its past is peppered with the names of monarchs, nobles, clerics and 'celebrities'. For most of the time it has been subsumed into the story of Twickenham, which in its turn was usually absorbed into the Domesday Book's Manor of Isleworth. The island has been owned in whole or in part by various English crowned heads, the nuns of Syon monastery in Isleworth, the Duke of Northumberland and the local parish, as well as a succession of innkeepers and businessmen. It is the only inhabited island in the Thames tideway between Teddington and the estuary, one of many facts that make it unique.

Nowadays it is a patchwork of small freeholds and leaseholds, but as recently as the early 1990s it was dominated, because largely owned, by a single person – the late Kingston-upon-Thames antique dealer, Michael Snapper. He was the last proprietor of the vanished hotel, whose site is now collectively owned by the residents of the Aquarius estate, and of the island's main path. He also owned the footbridge on to the island, which is today administered by a company owned by an island collective which bought him out. Two boating clubs and a couple of dozen businesses also own or lease property on the island, and about a score of houseboats are moored around it. It is therefore challenging to write a continuous narrative focused exclusively on the island – which has been described (by the inventor Trevor Baylis, its most famous resident), not without exaggeration, as '120 drunks clinging to a mudbank'. But it remains possible to trace much of its early history as an implicit, and occasionally explicit, part of the Manor of Isleworth-Syon, and later the Manor of Twickenham.

The tiny island has on occasion over the past half-millennium punched well above its minuscule weight in historical terms. For two decades from the early 1950s its hotel rose to world fame as a venue for jazz,

rhythm and blues and later pop, ending its days as a hippie colony until it went to pot, lost its liquor licence and caught fire. A surprisingly large number of people all over Britain and abroad remember Eel Pie Island's louche heyday, usually with a fond smile. The likes of Ken Colyer and Acker Bilk were followed by Long John Baldry and then the Rolling Stones and Rod Stewart, who made the place famous as they became famous themselves. Nor was the island merely a source of loud noises: the man who organised the music, the late Arthur Chisnall, ran a social and educational programme for young people alongside the concerts, which itself drew much attention at home and abroad.

Looking back to the end of the twentieth century, in fewer than thirty years the island was the scene of a huge fire (November 1996); its footbridge was undermined and replaced only after a mighty struggle with bureaucracy (1993–98), and its notorious hotel also burnt down (1971). In the earliest days of cinema, a studio on the island churned out comedies and spoofs featuring, among others, a certain Lieutenant Pimple, RN; some sixty years later, goosepimples featured prominently in pornographic films produced on an underheated boat in one of the island's yards.

Charles Dickens included the place in two of his novels in the mid nineteenth century, when Eel Pie Island was well established as a 'resort' for Londoners, who often arrived from the East End in pleasure steamers. Exiled French royals were the first presidents of the island-based Twickenham Rowing Club, one of the oldest and most distinguished in Britain. Before that, the island served as a playground for a doomed English royal duke; it boasted an inn and a bowling alley with a quoits court. And let us not forget the legend behind its bizarre name: Henry VIII's alleged taste for the eponymous delicacy from a local pie stall. None of this quite earns the little island a role in world history, but it is a most unusual place with a unique story, which these pages set out to tell.

OPPOSITE: Twickenham Rowing Club at high tide.

OVERLEAF: Dawn on the Thames.

Part 1

From the Stone Age to The Rolling Stones

Dan van der Vat

FROM THE ICE AGE TO ST BRIDGET

The Thames upstream of London flowed largely unconfined until Victorian times, when the mounting threat of flooding led to canalisation of the river by embankments. Ironically, subsequent construction on riverside land that used to be a natural flood plain increased the danger in the long term – as was shown, not for the first time, in the great flood of 1953. Much of the swollen waters by then had nowhere to go but on to built-up areas, a risk that was averted but not removed by the construction of the Thames Barrier at Woolwich in the 1970s.

In its natural state the river over many centuries threw up mudbanks or else carved parallel channels, especially on bends, creating islands at irregular intervals along much of its length. When William the Conqueror arrived in 1066, the Thames tideway – the stretch subject to the ebb and flow caused by sea tides – stopped near the Tower of London, which is why he built his fortress at that point. All but a millennium later the tideway stops at Teddington, two miles upstream from Eel Pie Island and more than a dozen from the Tower; it would go even further but for the lock and weir built there in 1811. Were it not for the Thames Barrier, Eel Pie Island would be flooded several times a year, more and more often, more and more deeply. It is also increasingly likely to flood from upstream as well. It would eventually have become uninhabitable. The other artificial constraint

now stopping the island from constantly changing its shape in the restless ebb and flow, as it used to, is the modern camp-shedding that acts like a corset and gives the island a neat, vertical edge.

Old maps show the island as an archipelago of three islets – or, strictly speaking, an archipotamo since this is a river and not the sea. A seventeenth-century map shows a lengthwise (east–west) division with the northern slice about half the width of the southern; and a breadthwise (north–south) division of the southern portion about one-third westward of the eastern tip. There is now no sign of the lengthwise division, while the breadthwise one has also been filled in but for a tiny creek that extends from the southern (mainstream) side of the island towards the middle. Before canalisation of the river and the construction of the half-lock at Richmond, which retains enough water to permit navigation between there and Teddington at low tide, it was possible on most days to walk dry-shod to the island at low tide. Even today, during the annual four-week draw-off in November decreed by the Port of London Authority, when Richmond Lock is left open, it is easy to walk across the river bed to the island at low tide (unless there has been heavy rainfall upstream). In 1830 the old London Bridge was demolished: with its many heavy piers, it had acted as a semi-dam. After this, the river was often all but emptied between Teddington to

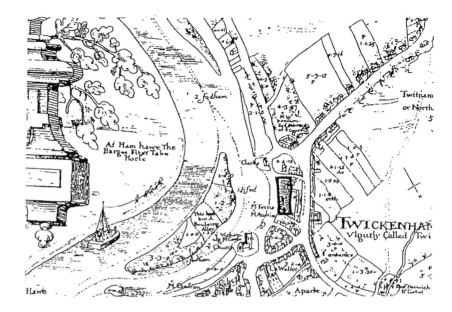

Richmond at low tide. Crossing to the island over the backwater was once facilitated by a causeway on piles with a sharp bend in the middle: it was probably built in the Stone Age and handily enabled the land to be used for grazing livestock without the need for boat or bridge. Spoil from the lock and weir and later dredging and anti-flood banking of the Thames consolidated the contemporary shape of the single island of Eel Pie. On a map it now looks more like a pie or Cornish pasty than ever.

The oldest recorded signs of human activity found on or close to Eel Pie Island include flint axes and pottery fragments dating back to about 3000 BC, Neolithic tools, a dagger blade, a spearhead and other bronze instruments. A small hoard of nine crude speculum (copper and tin alloy) coins was found on the island itself, dating back to the early Iron Age up to 2,600 years ago.

To say that the early history of Twickenham is patchy seriously understates the problem of the researcher whose attention is focused on only a small part of it. In 790 Offa, king of Saxon Mercia, granted a large area of local land to the Archbishop of Canterbury, and it changed hands between church and crown several times before the Conquest. We can safely assume that Eel Pie Island, as an appendage of the centre of Twickenham, was part of each transaction: it has always been part of Middlesex rather than Surrey on the opposite bank, from which it is divided

OPPOSITE: Looking across to the island at low tide during the annual draw-off, when Richmond Lock is left open, allowing the Thames to flow naturally.

by the mainstream. The backwater on the north side of the island thus also belongs to Twickenham. The island's official name was Twickenham Aight, Ait, Ayot, Ayte or Eyot; it was also referred to locally at various times as the Parish Ait, Goose Ait (the name of the vicar in 1635) and Osier Ait.

Twickenham was not named in the Domesday Book of 1086 because it was then part of the large Manor of Isleworth, awarded by William I soon after 1066 to Walter de St Valéry for his support during the Norman Conquest. Isleworth endured several territorial adjustments over the years. In 1301, for instance, Twickenham was formally attached (or re-attached) to it, one year after the Knights Templar briefly rented the local pastures for forty shillings, not long before they were disbanded. Under the Normans and the Plantagenets, ownership of the Manor passed back and forth between church, crown and nobility. In 1415 there occurred one of the most important events in local history when King Henry V founded a convent in the Manor of Isleworth. He named it Syon, a variant spelling of Zion, the biblical city of King David, and an early synonym for Jerusalem, which includes the original Mount Zion. The nuns who settled Syon belonged to an order founded by St Bridget (1304–72), a Swedish noblewoman who became a nun when widowed in 1344, soon forming her own small order, for which she was eventually canonised by the Pope. One of Henry's sisters

married the King of Sweden, which may explain why the English king endowed the order so generously.

Syon was the only Bridgettine foundation in Britain. It originally housed 60 nuns, with 25 monks to say Mass and administer the sacraments, including eight lay brothers to do the heavy work on the convent's lands. The convent prospered mightily from its endowment. It became known as the Manor of Isleworth-Syon and eventually included the whole of Twickenham. By 1431 the community had moved to the site of today's Syon House, owned by the Duke of Northumberland and built over the foundations of the once splendid abbey. The grazing on Eel Pie Island was for a time divided between Syon (two thirds) and the parish of Twickenham (one third), probably conforming with the old, lengthwise division of the island. One legend relating to the name of Eel Pie suggests that it was the monks of Syon who caught the eels and first put them in pies for sale in the Middle Ages.

DISSOLUTION

A turning point in the history of Twickenham, and with it Eel Pie Island (not to mention the whole of the rest of England and Wales), came with Henry VIII's dissolution of the monasteries in the 1530s. Meanwhile, a new entity, the Manor of Twickenham, had received its first mention in the 1440s. Hived off from Isleworth-Syon, it was formally known as the Manor

of Twickenham, Worton and Whitton. The lord of this manor in 1445–6 was a certain William York, of a family which had established itself in Twickenham on land leased from Syon Abbey around 1381. The new manor was recorded as 'Twickenham – York hold' and part of its land was sold to Henry Tudor, Earl of Richmond in Yorkshire, after he became King Henry VII, having claimed the throne in 1485 on his victory over Richard III, ending the Wars of the Roses. The family gave its name to the elegant seventeenth-century York House, opposite the island on the Middlesex bank, now the formal headquarters of the London Borough of Richmond-upon-Thames.

The history of Eel Pie Island is necessarily largely anecdotal, and one of the most poignant stories comes from the end of the seventeenth century. The royal Stuarts made much use of York House; Queen Anne (1665–1714), the last of that line to occupy the throne, lived there for many years before becoming queen in 1702. She married Prince Georg of Denmark and was pregnant 17 times, but only five babies were carried to full term and of those only one survived early infancy: William, and he lived only to the age of 11. Born in 1689, he was made Duke of Gloucester and was next in line to the throne after Anne, heir-apparent at the time. He spent much of his short life at York House, where the air was healthier than in London. The story goes that the sickly prince would round up his friends and take them to a piece

of open ground on Eel Pie Island, where he would parade them and march them up and down. This story is a vague echo of the tale of the 'Grand Old Duke of York' of nursery-rhyme fame, who marched his 10,000 men to the top of a hill and then down again. The Duke of York perpetrated this military blunder more than two centuries earlier, but the two stories have been confused. William died of hydrocephalus (water on the brain) in July 1700, two years before his mother became queen, thus depriving her of a direct heir.

Meanwhile, some time in the middle of the seventeenth century, Twickenham Ferry was inaugurated, the only Thames crossing upstream of Richmond Bridge for nearly three centuries in what is now the London Borough of Richmond. A rival ferry opened by Walter Hammerton in 1908 ousted the competition in 1915 in a legal battle that finished in the House of Lords. Nowadays the ferry, still known as Hammerton's, is a little further downstream than the original and does not call at the island. Access was via a chain-barge until the footbridge to Twickenham Embankment was built in 1957.

From about 1740 the island boasted a bowling alley with a court for quoits attached. The only other leisure facility in those days was an inn in a 'dingy wooden cottage' also described as 'an unassuming but popular little barn'. Called first the Ship Inn and later the White Cross, it dates from 1740 and was

ABOVE: An early pleasure-
steamer crosses to the island
hotel.

the first permanent building on the island. In his
Memorials of Twickenham (1872), the Rev. Richard
Cobbett, curate from 1865 to 1872 of St Mary's
Church, Twickenham, which faces the island, wrote:

> *The beautiful island called Twickenham Ayte,*
> *or Eel Pie Island, is deservedly a favourite*
> *resort for visitors and excursionists. The old*
> *house [the inn] . . . was taken down in 1830,*
> *and the present inn erected subsequently.*

The 'present inn', which indeed replaced the White
Cross in 1830, was the hotel, another important point
in island history. Whereas the old pub and bowling
alley were purely local facilities, the hotel turned the
island into a miniature resort, favoured by growing
numbers of Londoners who arrived on paddle-
steamers. Trippers would bring their own picnics and

'It had come to pass that afternoon that Miss Morleena
Kenwigs had received an invitation to repair next day,
per steamer from Westminster Bridge, unto the Eel-pie
Island at Twickenham: there to make merry upon a cold
collation, bottled beer, shrub and shrimps, and to dance
in the open air to the music of a locomotive band.'
Charles Dickens, 'Nicholas Nickleby', 1839

RIGHT: the extended Eel Pie Island Hotel in 1906. A third storey has been added, along with the huge ballroom in a separate building on the left.

BELOW: the original Eel Pie Island Hotel, c. 1830, painted by James Gooch just after it opened. Its elegance offers a stark contrast with the state of the building in its last days some 140 years later.

pay 6d each for access to the gardens, or else buy their food from the hotel, including the famous pies.

The hotel was opened and run by the Mayo family, formerly of the White Cross: first Thomas Mayo, then his brother James and later James's widow, Elizabeth. The paint was barely dry on the new building when it became the setting for a huge party to celebrate the birthday and accession to the throne of King William IV, on 23 August 1830. The event was held in the hotel and its grounds, which were lit up with coloured lamps and lanterns, as *The Times* reported on 25 August:

> *The walls and windows of Eel-pie-house were decorated with stars and crosses; and there was no lack of triumphal arches, to furnish which the neighbouring plantations had been robbed of their flowering shrubs . . . A floating car had been provided, in which Neptune, personated by an honest tar, in a Welsh wig, circum-navigated the island, drawn by dolphins and river horses, and attended by a respectable cortège of Naiads and Tritons. His marine majesty was towed along by King's watermen . . . and an excellent band of instrumentalists accompanied and imparted an additional charm to the watery triumph.*

The maritime theme was clearly inspired by the new monarch's attachment to the Royal Navy (he was known as the Sailor King) and the whole affair, which drew up to 600 people to the island, was the precursor of mighty celebrations to come, but nothing later quite matched the extravagance of the first time. Fireworks were set off and caused a fierce blaze (another portent) which damaged the hotel but was put out before most of the revellers noticed it; a panic would probably have been disastrous. The climax of the evening was a supper and ball 'which detained the party till an advanced hour in the morning'.

The hotel's popularity fluctuated: a handbook to London and its surroundings noted in 1876 that the island 'seems to have lost its power to attract excursionists'. In the great Thames flood of January 1877 the ground floor filled with water, the *Middlesex Chronicle* reporting that 'the pigs and calf have to be kept in an upstairs bedroom and the fowls are located in the drawing room'. Yet the trippers did keep coming in respectable numbers until war broke out in 1914 and punting on the Thames went out of fashion.

Leisure and pie-production were not the only industries on Eel Pie Island. The osiers, reeds and later willow trees that grew on and near the island were for centuries used to make baskets, and cages for fish and birds. The origin of the local boatbuilding tradition is not recorded but must go back at least three centuries. The main boatyard, and ancillary buildings for craftsmen, was opened in 1893 by Thames Electric and Motor Works Ltd; today, after many vicissitudes, Eel Pie Island Slipways Ltd (now belonging to Thames

RIGHT: Ken Dwan, who runs Eel Pie Island Slipways, is one of the most distinguished figures on the Thames. He is shown here on the left, wearing the cerise uniform of the Queen's Bargemaster, facing the Lord Lieutenant who is flanked by Beefeaters, at a ceremony at the Tower of London. Also in his wardrobe is the Doggett's Coat and Badge uniform, for which watermen still compete each year; and the bright red, Tudor-style outfit of a Thames Waterman.

Cruises and run by Ken Dwan, managing director and half-owner) uses the core of the original site as a boatyard. There will be more to say about boat-building in Part 3. To prevent the whole island from being swamped by industry, Twickenham Council, as it then was, insisted on preserving the views from upstream and downstream with trees at each end of the island; these wooded areas are now a wildlife sanctuary owned by Richmond Council.

The island was prominent in the early days of British cinema, when a 'studio' (in fact a hut) stood on part of the boatbuilding area at the north-eastern end. The moving spirit behind the Phoenix Film Company was Fred Evans (1889–1951), a music-hall comedian and childhood friend of Charlie Chaplin, whom he resembled when starring in his own films. His brother Joe wrote the 'scripts', including the inter-

titles between scenes of the silent two-reelers. Their output of some 200 films included, from 1912, a long series of mini-epics featuring Lieutenant Pimple, RN (played by Fred Evans), pastiches of a series about Lieutenant Darling, RN, made elsewhere in 1911–13. These included *Lieutenant Pimple's Dash for the Pole, Battle of Waterloo, Stolen Submarine, Charge of the Light Brigade* and, finally, in 1922, *Three Muske-teers*. The studio was producing six films a month, but a doubtless exhausted Fred Evans eventually returned to the music hall after his company went bankrupt. Lupino Lane was among the early stars who filmed on Eel Pie Island in a series of 'Kinekature' comedies.

THE FRENCH CONNECTION

Royalty took a hand once more in the history of Eel Pie Island and its environs in the middle of the nine-

ABOVE: The western tip of
Eel Pie Island showing one
of the nature reserves.

OPPOSITE: Inside the nature
reserve at the east end of the
island.

LEFT: York House,
Twickenham, once home
to British and French royalty,
now the home of the London
Borough of Richmond upon
Thames.

teenth century, when the tottering French monarchy finally fell. The last king, Louis-Philippe (1773–1850), lived in exile from 1793 to 1814, mostly in Twickenham; reigned from 1830 to 1848, then lived in exile once more, in Surrey, until his death. In 1854, the Duc d'Aumale, his fourth and youngest son, bought Orleans House, just off the eastern tip of the island, for his own lifelong exile. When Twickenham Rowing Club, third oldest on the Thames, was founded on the island in 1860, the duke was invited to become its first president, a post he held until his death in 1897; it was said that he used club business to mask his philandering. His eldest brother, Louis-Philippe, Comte de Paris and pretender to the French throne, bought York House on his marriage in 1864, lived there for seven years and sold it in 1876. One of his first acts was to give the Rowing Club the freehold of the land on which it stands today.

His son, also named Louis-Philippe and styled Duc d'Orleans, was born at York House in 1869 and bought it back in 1897. His decision to build a wall round its riverside garden, and his open support for the Boers in the South African War at the turn of the century, made him unpopular; in 1899 he was successfully sued by a local resident over a parcel of land on Eel Pie Island. Nevertheless, he briefly followed Aumale as president of the Rowing Club in 1897. He died in Sicily, a rather larger island, in 1926.

eel pie

Richmond Eel-pie

Skin, draw, & cleanse 2 good-sized Thames eels; trim off the fins, & cut them up in pieces about 3" long, & put these in a stewpan with 2 oz of butter, some chopped mushrooms, parsley, & a very little shalot, nutmeg, pepper & salt, 2 glasses of sherry, 1 of Harvey sauce, & barely enough water to cover the surface of the eels; let them on the fire, & as soon as they come to a boil, let them be removed, & the pieces of eels placed carefully in a pie dish; add 2 oz of butter, kneaded with 2 oz of flour, to the sauce; & having stirred it on the fire to thicken, add the juice of a lemon, & pour it over the pieces of eels in the pie dish; place some hard yolks of eggs on the top; cover with puff-paste; ornament the top; egg it over, bake for about an hour, & serve, either hot or cold.

LEGEND AND EEL PIES

The story goes that King Henry VIII was overcome by hunger one day on his way upstream in the royal barge from London to Hampton Court, the fabulous palace built by Cardinal Thomas Wolsey, his Lord Chancellor. On his way past the island, he is said to have stopped the barge, sent a minion ashore to buy him an eel pie from the famous stall run by a 'Mistress Mayo', acquired a taste for her pies and then frequently indulged it. This tale is highly suspicious: the Eel Pie Island Hotel was built by the owners of the White Cross inn, the Mayo family – but in 1830, not 1530! Elizabeth Mayo, the real 'Mistress Mayo', died in 1895 at the age of 95; she is buried with her husband and family in the graveyard at Oak Lane, Twickenham. And local historians have found no trace of the name Eel Pie Island earlier than the end of the eighteenth century.

Be that as it may, it was reported in local and national newspapers in May 1923 that a '400-year-old tradition' was revived when world-champion sculler Ernest Berry, in the full Tudor-style scarlet uniform of a Thames Waterman, handed over an eel pie, described as the first of the season, to a man dressed as Henry VIII and accompanied by 'Queen Catherine'. Reports referred to 'the ancient ceremony of "landing the pie" . . . founded during the reign of Henry VIII, which has not been observed for over a century'. The custom was said to have been aban-

doned early in the nineteenth century, when the deranged George III banished his queen, Charlotte, from Kew Palace to Twickenham. The 1923 stunt appears to have been an isolated event. Diligent research has failed to show that the royal pie tradition ever existed, certainly not as far back as Tudor times, although old maps appear to show a kiosk on the island, separate from the inn – the 'famous pie stall', no doubt. We have already noted that the island is shaped like a pie, and that eels used to be caught there. The legend of hungry Henry, prince of pie-fanciers, makes a nice story. Modern local attempts to make eel pies from 'traditional' recipes have sometimes turned out to be all but unfit for human consumption . . .

ISLAND FOR SALE

Parts of Eel Pie Island, mainly the hotel and the principal boatyard (divided into three plots in the 1980s), were put up for sale from time to time. Within four years of Mrs Mayo's death, the hotel was on offer in January 1899 at an auction house in the City of London. It went for £4,700, which was seen as rather low, considering that 'the buyer takes over a fully licensed hotel and grounds', as the *Richmond and Twickenham Times* observed. In September of the same year furniture, crockery, cutlery, glass, a 50-foot marquee and 'a brilliant-tone cottage pianoforte' came under the hammer of a Hounslow auctioneer

who visited the island for the sale. The hotel itself was put up for sale again in August 1919 by another City of London auctioneer. Facilities at that time included 14 bedrooms, various sitting rooms and lounges, with other rooms and tea gardens in extensive grounds. The boatyard was auctioned in October 1906, when Joseph Mears acquired it from Thames Electric and Motor Works.

Over the turn of the nineteenth century, the first dwelling-houses began to appear on the north side of the island. Mostly made of wood and still extant, some of these little 'holiday' cottages, according to local lore, were occupied by the mistresses of local businessmen. Some have been completely rebuilt or even replaced. A handful of more modern dwellings, mostly built in conventional brick, were added during the twentieth century, but the main residential development occurred in the 1970s on the site of the island hotel (see Part 3). The prettiest of the older dwellings is generally held to be Hurley Cottage, which is rather larger than it looks from the main island path; its white clapboard walls gleam warmly behind its immaculate front garden. House names combine the suburban with the exotic; the architecture embraces the banal and the adventurous: The Nook, Sunrise, Jacob's Ladder (formerly Mascot), Ripple (being rebuilt), Wyndfall, Wild Thyme, Desdemona, The Cottage, Kingslee (formerly the unpronounceable Hluwhluwe), Copper Beech . . . These

THE
"ISLAND HOTEL,"
(Lice... the White Cross Hotel),
...IE ISLAND,
...KENHAM,

...dens, the br... avenue leading to the Hotel, and
...about three ... a charming position in
...ver with ... Backwater,
...the Met...
...mmon
...tel w...

TWICKENHAM.

To Brewers, Distillers, Wine and Spirit Merchants, Hotel Proprietors, AND OTHERS.

PARTICULARS AND CONDITIONS OF SALE

OF THE WELL-KNOWN

VALUABLE FREEHOLD PROPERTY

DISTINGUISHED AS

"EEL PIE ISLAND,"

Which occupies a unique position on the River Thames, with Landing Stages from both shores,

COMPRISING

THE HOTEL,

Which is Fully Licensed, and has also a Music and Dancing License in addition, with the Out-buildings

AND THE

CHARMING PLEASURE GROUNDS AND GARDENS,

In all about 3a. 3r. 13p.;

THE VALUABLE GOODWILL WILL BE INCLUDED IN THE SALE;

Which will be Sold by Auction, by

MR. MASON

At the Mart, Tokenhouse Yard, E.C.,

ON THURSDAY, JANUARY THE 12TH, 1899,

AT TWO o'CLOCK PRECISELY.

Particulars and Conditions of Sale may be obtained of Messrs. CRIDLAND & NELL, Solicitors, 27, Bedford Row, W.C.; and of Mr. MASON, Estate Agent and Auctioneer, WINDSOR (and Ascot).

WILLMORE AND SCOTT, PRINTERS, WINDSOR.

TWICKENHAM.

Particulars and Conditions of Sale

OF THE VERY VALUABLE

FREEHOLD

WITH POSSESSION

OF THAT CELEBRATED PROPERTY KNOWN AS THE

"ISLAND HOTEL,"

(Licensed as the White Cross Hotel),

EEL PIE ISLAND,

TWICKENHAM,

Together with the well laid out Tea Gardens and Grounds.

Which will be Sold by Public Auction, by

MESSRS. HASLETT

AT WINCHESTER HOUSE, OLD BROAD STREET, E.C.,

On THURSDAY, AUGUST 28th, 1919,

AT ONE O'CLOCK PRECISELY.

(Unless previously sold.)

May be viewed by Cards from the Auctioneers. Printed Particulars and Conditions of Sale may be obtained at the place of Sale; of Messrs. SAYLE, CARTER & Co., Solicitors, 35 Queen Victoria Street, E.C.; and at the

Auctioneers' Offices, 36 & 37 Queen Street, Cheapside, E.C. 4

TWO HOTEL ENTRANCES, SPACIO... ...UNGES,
BUFFET, PRETTILY DESIGNED ...OOKING
THE RIVER, SERVICE BAR, ... STILL
ROOM, DRYING ROOM, KN... ...ES' AND
GENTLEMEN'S LA...

In the Basement—

CONCRETED CELLARAGE, LARDER AND WORKSHO...

ABOVE: *Richmond Yacht Club.*

OPPOSITE: *Advertisements for various sales of the 'Island Hotel'.*

line the north of the side path, while Kent Lodge, The Haven, Kuala Lumpur, Blinkwater, Hurley Cottage, Min y Don and Ivy Castle are among the properties on the main path leading to Aquarius. The Rowing Club, which had opened with a floating boathouse, acquired its present land-based premises just before the end of the nineteenth century. The Richmond Yacht Club (which is neither in Richmond nor a yacht club, but is really the Twickenham cruiser-club) was opened in 1934 and owns a clubhouse, built in 1968

on land donated by Michael Snapper, which is often used for island social events.

The main industrial activity on the island before and after the Second World War was boatbuilding and maintenance. No boats are built there now, but there is still industrial activity. Mike Keep recalled his childhood on the island immediately after the war, when his father Jeff, a publican, took over the hotel. Mike and his brother John had the run of the island and a resident donkey as a playmate:

'By the riverside were landing-craft which had been moored up after the invasion of France. We went to a primary school in Twickenham, crossing to the mainland by ferry-boat' Mike & John Keep, recalling their childhood on the island

RIGHT: This literary curiosity is an American crime novel in a wartime economy paperback edition, on sale in the early 1940s (it was originally published in 1933). David Frome was a pseudonym used by an American author, Mrs Zenith Brown, for her UK-based mysteries. She shows a detailed knowledge of Eel Pie Island and its Twickenham environs, as well as of the Metropolitan Police. A body is found on an island beach: enter Chief Inspector Bull of Scotland Yard . . . The appeal of the island as a setting for fictional crime was enhanced in June 1948, when a long-running American radio series of newly invented 'Sherlock Holmes' stories broadcast an episode entitled 'The Complicated Poisoning at Eel Pie Island'.

LEFT: Eel Pie Island is home to a variety of craft, large and small.

OVERLEAF: An eager crowd pack the Eel Pie Jazz Club.

There was a boathouse in the grounds which was apparently used as an early movie-film studio in the Chaplin era. There was a ball-room with enormous light-shades that were lowered to the floor for cleaning. As kids we used them as 'wigwams'. Eel pies were available then, I remember, but I wasn't tempted.

The last owner of the Eel Pie Island Hotel was Michael Snapper (1908–2006), an antique dealer based since before the Second World War at Kingston-upon-Thames, a few miles upstream of the island whose history he dominated for a quarter of a century. He acquired the premises in 1951, and in May 1952 registered a company called Eel Pie Entertainments. He and Cyril Anthony Croot owned equal shares; they and their wives were listed as directors, with Croot living on the premises as hotel manager. After the company was dissolved in October 1958 for failing to submit accounts, Snapper retained the freehold of the hotel and grounds. It was under his tutelage that the musical history of Eel Pie Island took off.

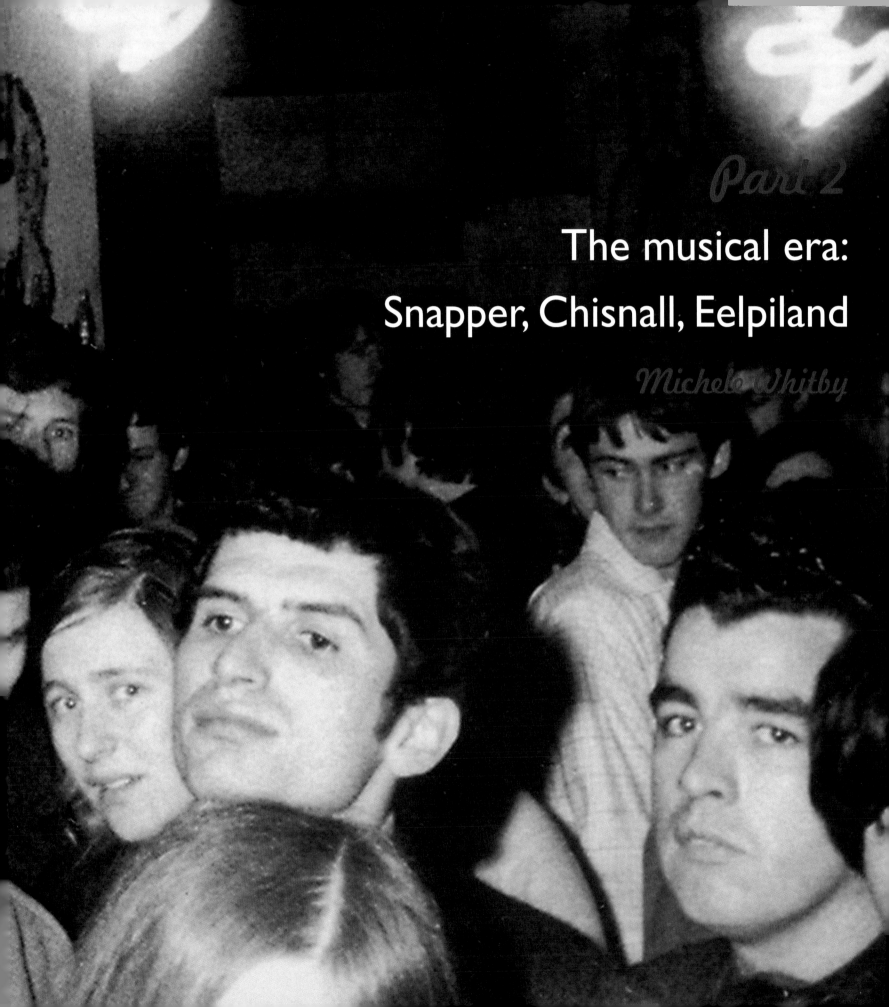

Part 2

The musical era:
Snapper, Chisnall, Eelpiland

Michele Whitby

BELOW: Michael Snapper and his wife dress the part for the London to Brighton Rally. Snapper had a passion for vintage cars.

ABOVE: The Eel Pie Island Hotel in the Fifties. John Winstone, who helped Arthur Chisnall set up the early parties, wrote to the local student unions on 30 May 1956: 'As many of the students are already aware, the inevitable party will be held at Eel Pie Island this Friday 1/6/56 with the Terra Buona Jazz Band playing for dancing, followed by a Skiffle Group, who will play until their audience has fallen exhausted. There will be a charge of 1/6d to cover expenses, and membership passports will cost 2/6d. We anticipate that after 3 weeks entrance will be by Passport only, as the Hall is not of infinite size.'

SNAPPER MOVES IN

In the early 1950s Kingston-upon-Thames became home to the entrepreneurial Michael Snapper. Born in 1908 to a family of Chelsea-based antique dealers, Snapper – who, according to his son Emile, 'could barely read or write and lived like a king but dressed like a tramp' – began his working life in his father's shop and before long was running his own King's Road business. He grew into an extraordinarily exuberant man, counting among his numerous passions ice-skating, water-skiing, horse-riding and vintage cars. He dabbled in the entertainment business, performing with his dog, the 'World Champion Jumper' Mikeve (once the world record-holder for the highest canine leap), and also bought a bear with the overambitious intention of teaching it to ice-skate; it reportedly ended up sharing the flat above his shop.

After the Second World War, he sold the Chelsea shop to open 'Snapper's Corner' in London Road, Kingston, where he and his new wife also lived. His enthusiasm for the river and boating led him to become a founder member and First Commodore of the London River Yacht Club in 1950. While searching for suitable club headquarters, he recalled childhood jaunts for Sunday afternoon tea on Eel Pie Island. Thinking this might be the ideal spot for the Yacht Club, he ventured across the water on the little chain ferry one day in 1952 and somehow ended up buying the rather grand Eel Pie Island Hotel.

The building came complete with half a dozen or so resident 'odd people'. Arthur Chisnall, who was working for Michael at Snapper's Corner, recollected:

A Russian countess, along with her secretary and chauffeur, lived there. Some funds would arrive from an unknown source every few months; they would all disappear for a while and return when the money ran out, to stay on tick at the hotel. The next cheque would arrive and they'd pay up as little as they could get away with and clear off to the West End or somewhere. And a chap known as Cockles who (funnily enough) ran the cockle and whelk stall on the mainland, he lived there too.

At the time, the hotel was providing weekly entertainment, described by Chisnall as 'a rather washed-out trio playing quicksteps, fox-trots and what not to about half a dozen people'. A supper licence allowed the hotel to serve after-hours drinks with meals, but people were hardly going there for the food. The police cottoned on and, none too happy about illegal liquor sales, caused the licence to be withdrawn. This, according to Arthur, 'made the difference between the books barely balancing and not balancing at all'. The time was clearly ripe for something new and inspired to rejuvenate the old timbers.

Antique dealing aside, Chisnall's true vocation lay in social research, his particular interest being to

RIGHT: Arthur Chisnall in the early Sixties.

identify society's 'trend-forming groups' especially among the new-fangled 'problem teenagers'. He told me: 'It seemed quite rational to me that we should be able to find a trend-forming group. And it's obvious, I think, that if you can locate such a group you can predict and plan for possible problems.' The early 1950s saw Arthur intuitively pick up on the direction-less mood that was unsettling many youngsters. Having in so many cases spent their early, formative years in dispersed families while their parents fought the war, young people lacked any strong or binding culture to relate to as a group. To many, churches no longer seemed relevant, and neither were the youth clubs. Citing the example of Kingston's YMCA, with its single billiard table covered in a shoddy baize substitute that made for terrible play, Arthur sighed, 'and *that* was the entertainment in Kingston!', his tone of voice implying the inevitability of major change on the horizon. These were the incipient rumblings of the 'youthquake' and Chisnall had his finger on its pulse from the start.

Through working in Snapper's Kingston antiques emporium, Arthur quickly identified the local art students as his trend-forming group. His conversations with them led him to the natural conclusion that what they really needed was 'a place to get together, make a little noise and dance to it'. Since I spent my own youth soaking up London's more-than-abundant nightlife, Arthur's comment, at first, sounded so

obvious and unremarkable that it was difficult to appreciate the thinking behind it, so innovative at the time. I had to remind myself that in the 1950s teenagers and all their associated problems were a newborn phenomenon. As Arthur put it: 'Before the war, people seemed to go from childhood straight to adulthood – from short pants to long.' Now, suddenly, Britain's newly refloated post-war boat was being rocked by a novel brand of citizen. Rather than attempt to make provision for them, mainstream society recoiled with horror. Without sympathetic, innovative thinkers such as Arthur Chisnall, life for some of the frustrated youth of south-west London and beyond might have turned out very differently.

Snapper, meanwhile, was keen to breathe new life into his riverside venue. Had it not been for the obstacle of a council refusal and the outrage of island residents, he would have built an outdoor roller-skating rink on the site and had the ballroom converted into a Monte Carlo-style casino. These grand schemes not being to local tastes, he allowed Arthur, who had wartime experience of organising jazz concerts, and some of his pals to use the ballroom to host parties. Early 1956 saw the first of many shindigs held there, initially free of charge and only advertised by word of mouth. One of the group of hell-raisers, John Winstone, recalled their success:

We had to start charging a door fee after the first few events, to pay for repairs and, of

LEFT: Snaps from the family album: Snapper with his champion dog, Mikeve, ice-skating, and enjoying the fair with his son Emile.

'My first memories are crossing the river in a punt; many used to fall into the river even before they'd started on the scrumpy. Later came a little rickety bridge, which spoilt it all a bit, and we used to give Min sixpence for going over it (she was a little lady and the Goons were in full swing at the time; everybody was called Min!). Those were definitely the fun days. I lived and breathed **trad jazz** and would go home with very sore, dirty feet from jiving to Monty Sunshine's music and lots of others just starting out. I taught my older brother to jive and we would go to Eel Pie together, skip-jiving our feet off!' Gaynor Gadd (Young)

'We were amazed at the popularity of the first event. We had expected a few dozen; it turned out to be hundreds, which tested the bouncing floor somewhat' John Winstone, recalling the first free island gig in 1956

course, the bands, who wanted a little more than the traditional crate of beer. I knew Acker [Bilk] from Bristol and tried the crate of beer trick on him – unsuccessfully! After a few weeks we were able to give Michael Snapper £3 per week in rent. I was treasurer of sorts for a while, looking after the take of one shilling and sixpence a head.

Word spread fast on the grapevine and within a few weeks there were, as Arthur told me with a mischievous chuckle, 'hundreds of art students, beatniks, jazz buffs and plain old pleasure-seekers who, having discovered Eel Pie Island, never really went away for the next eleven years!'

The regularity of the events soon prompted the local police to ask Arthur to form a proper club with a membership list. It made complete sense to them to let the parties continue, albeit on a more formal basis. Their job would be made easier if all these new-fangled teenagers were under one roof: that way they knew where to look for them.

Although the ravers attending these free parties had a ball, they were starting to ask to see some different bands, while the bands themselves, despite their love of playing there, thought it would be even better if they could get paid a decent rate. Formation of the Eel Pie Jazz Club with a paying membership solved all these problems – the police were happy, the bands and the audience were happy, and so was

Michael Snapper, who could now make some regular rent from the ballroom.

So on Friday 10 August 1956 the official 'Guest Register for Eelpiland Jazz Club' was set up. Ken Colyer, a name that soon became synonymous with the island, provided the entertainment, the first band to do so professionally. All this heralded eleven years of partying in the middle of the Thames at Twickenham. Membership cards were issued bearing the legend 'Passport to Eelpiland' and giving each bearer 'any assistance he/she might require in his/her lawful business of Jiving and generally Cutting a Rug'.

Rock 'n' Roll had already crossed the Atlantic. Elvis, with swivelling hips and suggestively curled lip, was shocking the nation's parents and cruising up the charts with 'Heartbreak Hotel', but revivalist jazz (or trad jazz as it became generally known) was the music of choice for the group Arthur considered the 'trend formers', essentially an art-school crowd of bohemians and beatniks. Emulating the styles and sounds of the New Orleans Dixieland jazz popularised in the United States during the early twentieth century, early British exponents such as Humphrey Lyttleton, Chris Barber, Alex Welsh, Cy Laurie and Ken Colyer had been devotees since the mid 1940s. The Eel Pie Hotel ballroom timbers vibrated to the upbeat, swinging sound of trumpets, trombones, clarinets, banjos and the big bass drum, while duffel-coated and bearded (if you were male, obviously)

OPPOSITE: Ken Colyer was a regular performer at Eelpiland throughout its eleven-year history.

OVERLEAF: Membership applications, 'passports' and advertisements from the heyday of Eelpiland.

EEL PIE ISLAND HOTEL
TWICKENHAM
—

Eelpiland presents
for Passport Holders and Guests

Fri.	Sept.	12	Don Steele
Sat.	„	13	Micky Ashma
Fri.	„	19	Mike Peters (E
Sat.	„	20	Acker Bilk
Fri.	„	26	Dave Nelson
Sat.	„	27	Graham Stew
Fri.	Oct.	3	Teddy Layto
Sat.	„	4	Terry Lightfo
Fri.	„	10	Ian Bell
Sat.	„	11	Alex Welsh

(Notes overleaf)

EEL PIE ISLAND HOTEL
TWICKENHAM
—

Eelpiland presents
for Passport Holders and Guests

Fri.	Feb.	15th	Clyde Valley Stompers
Sat.	Feb.	16th	Ian Bell
Fri.	Feb.	22nd	Alex Welsh
Sat.	Feb.	23rd	Piltdown Seven
Thursday	Feb.	28th	Ken Colyer
Sat.	Mar.	2nd	Ian Bell
Fri.	Mar.	8th	Crane River
Fri.	Mar.	15th	Dave Carey
Sat.	Mar.	16th	Sandy Brown

E. S. O. B. R. M.

State of NERVOUSNESS
Bureau of NUISANCES

LICENSE NUMBER 8846
THE COMMISSIONER ALREADY HAS YOUR NUMBER. BUT WE'VE ASSIGNED THIS ONE TO YOU ANY WAY

BACK SEAT DRIVERS LICENSE

PRINT IN FULL

ADDRESS

CITY   ZONE   STATE

This is to certify that the person herein named has passed all tests for nervousness and has been licensed to irritate, annoy, criticize, and otherwise disturb the operator of the car

SIGNATURE OF LICENSEE

DATE ISSUED 1952
THIS LICENSE GOOD FOR "THE REST OF YOUR LIFE"

ISSUED BY
Hugo Blow, S.S.C.
COMMISSIONER OF NERVOUS WRECKS
DEPT. OF INTERIOR CONFUSION

BACK SEAT DRIVER OTHERWISE MUST KEEP QUIET WHILE VEHICLE IS IN MOTION

WE request and require in the name of His Excellency PRINCE PAN all those whom it may concern to give the bearer of this passport ....

Jack Tocock

any assistance he/she may require in his/her lawful business of jiving and generally cutting a rug.

GIVEN UNDER OUR HAND THIS 1ST. DAY OF SEPTEMBER 1963

PAN

PRINCE OF TRADS

MICHAEL SNAPPER
invites you to the
Opening Night Dance of the
"HACIÉNDA" BALLROOM
EEL PIE ISLAND HOTEL
TWICKENHAM

Sunday, 1st December 1957
at 8 p.m.

A well-known Dance Band
Also a celebrated Caribean Steel Band

DRESS OPTIONAL   TICKET ADMITS TWO

EEL PIE ISLAND HOTEL
TWICKENHAM
—

Eelpiland presents
for Passport Holders and Guests

Sat.	Oct.	25	Graham Stewart
Fri.	„	31	Dave Nelson
Sat.	Nov	1	Acker Bilk
Fri.	„	7	Brian Taylor
Sat.	„	8	Wally Fawkes
Fri.	„	14	Micky Ashman
Sat.	„	15	Sandy Brown / Al Fairweather
Fri.	„	21	Mole Ben
Sat.	„	22	Micky Ashman
Fri.	„	28	Pete Wells Benefit

(late night—details to follow)

(Notes overleaf)

Record Rendezvous
RECORD & COFFEE BAR

Junction of Church Terrace and Red Lion Street, Richmond

Harmoniously Blended Bach Steaks.   Trad Coffee

Brubeck Sandwiches (non B.R. type)   Lyon Type Eggs and Hamlet.   Chopin Salad

Mixed Gorilla in Antique Cage (modernised)

Served by Artistically Designed Keepers at non-Ruinous Prices

---

EEL PIE ISL
TWICKE
—

Eelpilan
for Passport Ho

Fri.	Jan. 17	A
Sat.	Jan. 18	M
Fri.	Jan. 24	M
also Sandy Pa		
American		
Sat.	Jan. 25	S
Fri.	Jan. 31	A
Sat.	Feb. 1	L
Fri.	Feb. 7	D
Sat.	Feb. 8	A
Fri.	Feb. 14	T
Sat.	Feb. 15	A
Fri.	Feb. 21	
Sat.	Feb. 22	

EEL PIE ISLAND HOTEL
TWICKENHAM
—

Eelpiland presents
for Passport Holders and Guests

Fri.	Aug.	16th	Graham Stewart
Sat.	Aug.	17th	Merseysippi
Fri.	Aug.	23rd	Storyville
Sat.	Aug.	24th	Acker Bilk
Thursday	Aug.	29th	Ken Colyer
Fri.	Aug.	30th	Storyville
Sat.	Aug.	31st	Ian Bell
Fri.	Sept.	6th	Storyville
Sat.	Sept.	7th	Sandy Brown
Fri.	Sept.	13th	Jubilee

E. S. O. B. R. M.

We request and require in the name of His Excellency Prince Pan all those whom it may concern to give the Bearer of this Passport

....

any assistance he/she may require in his/her lawful business of Jiving and generally Cutting a Rug.

Given under our Hand this 1st day of August, 1967,

PAN
PRINCE OF TRADS

EEL PIE ISLAND HOTEL
TWICKENHAM
—

Eelpiland presents
for Passport Holders and Guests

Fri.	Oct.	25th	Jubilee
Sat.	Oct.	26th	Ian Bell
Fri.	Nov.	1st	Sonny Morris
Sat.	Nov.	2nd	Sandy Brown
Fri.	Nov.	8th	Ian Bell
Sat.	Nov.	9th	Alex Welsh
Fri.	Nov.	15th	Temperance 7 and Jamaican Steel Band
Sat.	Nov.	16th	Terry Lightfoot
Fri.	Nov.	22nd	Mike Peters
Sat.	Nov.	23rd	Bruce Turner
Fri.	Nov.	29th	Don Steele's Jazzmen

E. S. O. B. R. M.

Passport
TO
EELPILAND

No. 12303

Guests

gan

s

Caroline

wn

ther

eanais

esworth

lk Song

rs

clude six

eather

1 APPLICATION FOR MEMBERSHIP

OF

THE EELPILANDERS

I _J. S. Chint_ OF _10 Flower House_
Flower Rd. Kingst ~~ISH TO~~ BECOME A
MEMBER OF THE EELPILANDERS . I AM NOT UNDER 18 YEARS OF AGE . IF
ACCEPTED I AGREE TO OBEY THE RULES & REGULATIONS OF THE CLUB AS
LAID DOWN FROM TIME TO TIME . I SUBMIT 2/6d AS REGISTRATION FEE.

J. Chint signature

W. Stuart. Rae.

Tom Carroll

R. W. Wilkes.

2 APPLICATION FOR MEMBERSHIP

OF

THE EELPILANDERS

I _J. R. W. Wilkes._ OF _56 Portland Avenue._
New Malden. Surrey. ~~WISH TO~~ BECOME A
MEMBER OF THE EELPILANDERS . I AM NOT UNDER 18 YEARS OF AGE . IF
ACCEPTED I AGREE TO OBEY THE RULES & REGULATIONS OF THE CLUB AS
LAID DOWN FROM TIME TO TIME . I SUBMIT 2/6d AS REGISTRATION FEE .

R. W. Wilkes. signature

3 _Tom Carroll_

W. Stuart-Rae _J. Chint_

APPLICATION FOR MEMBERSHIP

OF

THE EELPILANDERS

I _T. W. Carroll_ OF _50 Bransby Rd_
Chessington Surrey. ~~WISH TO~~ BECOME A
MEMBER OF THE EELPILANDERS . I AM NOT UNDER 18 YEARS OF AGE . IF
ACCEPTED I AGREE TO OBEY THE RULES & REGULATIONS OF THE CLUB AS
LAID DOWN FROM TIME TO TIME . I SUBMIT 2/6 d AS REGISTRATION FEE .

T. W. Carroll signature

W. Stuart Rae.

J. Chint

R. W. Wilkes.

J. Chint

OPPOSITE: 'Fluff' at
Eelpiland, 1963: 'Arthur
was always there to chat
and help us if we had any
concerns in life. He gave
us his time.'

'We dressed down, in dark clothes, wore our hair long and put on layers of mascara. I used to come on the 667 trolley bus, go over the bridge and pay my 4d toll to the two old ladies, and then as I walked through the trees I'd hear it – the trumpet and trombone – and I'd break into a run, I couldn't get there quick enough.

'We drank Newcastle Brown Ale, trying to make one bottle last all night as we had very little money to spend, and anyway alcohol wasn't a necessity. Later in the evening we'd all come out, **hot and exhausted** from dancing. My hair used to be all wet and I was positively steaming. I remember it being absolutely packed when the Temperance Seven played – people on other people's shoulders. And I'd be in a filthy temper because there was no room to dance!' *Heather White, aka 'Fluff'*

punters stomped and jived to the strains of 'Tin Roof Blues' and 'Tiger Rag'.

From the outset the club was special. Situated as it was in a building of faded opulence, looking like something from *Gone With the Wind* right in the middle of the Thames, it already had a head start on any run-of-the-mill pub function room. Clarinettist Bill Greenow, who played with the Brent River Jazz Band, described his memories of seeing Eel Pie Island for the first time in 1954, having cycled from Gunnersbury, west London, to take a dip at Twickenham Baths.

What a mysterious place it looked! It was completely covered in trees and undergrowth with lots of old buildings clinging to the ground by the water's edge. About three years later I started playing there and, well, at the time you don't realise what you've got, but looking back on it all Eel Pie was the most unique place, all the murals on the walls, the arches and dusty atmosphere. After the austerity of the war years the bohemian freedom we found there was a breath of fresh air. We weren't rebels, as in carrying knives or such like; it was a musical rebellion against the Dance Hall era and the staidness of the BBC.

As already noted, the first band to be formally booked to play the Eel Pie Jazz Club was the much-lauded Ken Colyer's Jazzmen. One evening while setting up, the Guv'nor, as Ken was known, remarked to his band that the atmosphere on the island was straight out of New Orleans. And if anyone knew, Ken did. The obsessive trumpeter was well respected among the jazz crowd for his supreme dedication to the authentic New Orleans sound. In 1952 while in the Merchant Navy he had jumped ship in Mobile, Alabama, and hopped on a Greyhound bus to the hallowed city of New Orleans, to hang out and play with his heroes.

He spent a blissful month or so in the 'Big Easy', indulging his musical passions by playing and even recording with old masters such as Emile Barnes, Percy Humphrey and George Lewis (who would later tour Britain with Colyer) before he was arrested and thrown into prison. Incarcerated for the technicality of overstaying his visa, Colyer was told word had gone round that he was a 'nigger lover'. This being Fifties Louisiana, epicentre of Southern discrimination, state law forbade white and coloured musicians to share a stage – a regulation Colyer had openly flouted. Even the prison was racially segregated, but at least Colyer spent his 38 cell-bound days buoyed by the hundreds of voices harmoniously drifting across the jail yard from the 'colored wing', sometimes joyous and rocking, sometimes wailing the blues, but always an inspirational solace.

Having left England a virtual unknown, he returned a year later almost a legend; trad jazz had

'For some reason my parents didn't seem to mind me going to the island. What I didn't realise was that they knew Arthur and had him keeping a watchful eye on me!' 'Fluff'

'This is as close as you will get to New Orleans in England, the atmosphere and the feel is here. I have never experienced it so strongly anywhere else'
Ken Colyer

'It was a great club with an enthusiastic audience — so much so that when they started dancing the floor was like an ocean wave, going up and down at least a foot'
Acker Bilk

'**I didn't go for the bands**; I went for the beer – Newcastle Brown. I knew the bouncers so I got in even though I was under age. There was a bowler hat behind the bar – they used to say **it was Acker Bilk's**. The bar was OK, but the ballroom was a dive!'
Ted Leppard, formerly of Eel Pie Slipways

'You could almost see the sex rising – like steam from a kettle. It suited us randy young musicians extremely well. It was very difficult not to get laid on Eel Pie Island' George Melly

OPPOSITE: Ken Colyer (above) and Acker Bilk (below) were among the many well-respected jazz musicians to perform on Eel Pie Island.

been gathering momentum while he was away and *Melody Maker* had picked up his New Orleans exploits. Letters smuggled out of prison via his brother Bill made their way on to its pages and his incarceration became front-page news. He stepped off the boat-train at Waterloo station to be met by his brother Bill along with Chris Barber and Monty Sunshine, and he was more than ready to join their band. He had already fully earned the respect of fans and fellow musicians alike.

Colyer was the first of many eminent names to play the island. Cy Laurie, George Melly, Diz Disley, Eric Silk, the Temperance Seven, Acker Bilk, Kenny Ball and various band leaders with 'stompers', New Orleans or otherwise, were among the countless jazzmen who followed in Colyer's footsteps to enthrall the skip-jiving crowds in the Eel Pie ballroom. Acker Bilk played there many times with his Paramount Jazz Band and remembered having to haul huge drums across the bridge, which always seemed to him somewhat unfair seeing as his own instrument was a small, light clarinet:

> I recollect a smartly dressed pin-striped gentleman who stood in front of the bands – conducting! Needless to say us jazz musicians took no notice of him whatsoever.

George Melly recollected his discovery of Eel Pie Island by way of an advertisement for a 'Grand Jazz Ball with Cy Laurie' in the *Melody Maker*, as told in the third part of his spirited autobiography *Owning Up*:

> I hadn't heard Cy Laurie at the time, but I liked the sound of Eel Pie Island. It seemed to go with 'Gut Bucket' or 'Honky Tonk'. It had the right feel to it. It not only sounded right, it looked right too.

George was intrigued enough to venture along to the 'Grand Jazz Ball' which, as it turned out, wasn't all that grand: 'I think the band was almost as big as the audience!' Melly commented, adding that this was, however, 'in those days a perfectly respectable number'. He stayed and sank a few pints then asked Cy Laurie if he could get up and sing; several tunes later he was asked to join the band. Melly's first Eel Pie experience had led to him going home 'in a state of hysterical happiness': he had become a singer in a proper jazz band! He went on to perform there on many occasions.

In those very early pre-footbridge days of the Eel Pie Jazz Club, a small, precarious ferryboat was the only means of getting across to the hotel. Many musicians remember making the hazardous trip across the Thames, cramming themselves, their instruments and girlfriends into the boat in anticipation of the great evening ahead. Perilous enough in sober daylight, stepping aboard on the way home after a few pints was even more so. Trumpeter and photographer Mike Peters, who regularly played at Eel Pie with his band

THESE PAGES (clockwise from top left): Champion Jack Dupree on stage; girls getting in the groove; another packed house; getting friendly in the alcoves; soaking up the atmosphere.

RIGHT: The boys watch the girls . . .

the New Orleans Stompers, described it as 'a decidedly dodgy affair, like the D-Day landings but without the gunfire'. Amazingly there is no record of any major mishap among the musicians, but it would be no surprise to discover the odd clarinet or trumpet buried in the mud beneath the river.

BATTLE FOR EELPILAND

Arthur Chisnall steadily built up the club's reputation as a jazz hot spot, despite the fact that the only advertising took the form of a slip of paper a mere couple of inches wide and a notice-board detailing up-and-coming bands. For over six months he had successfully held parties every Friday and Saturday night; then, out of the blue early in 1957, he suddenly faced a takeover bid. Michael Snapper had apparently approached Don Kingswell and the Cy Laurie Agency with a view to them using the ballroom on a full-time basis. Arthur was furious; he had an agreement with Snapper, albeit a verbal one, to use the ballroom until Easter at least, and was incensed about the prospect of being squeezed out of his own club. Having received a letter stating that the Cy Laurie Club was now in charge, Arthur, in typical dauntless style, came up with an inspired plan for a counter-attack. Faced with a double-booked evening – Chisnall had the Omega Jazz Band and Kingswell the Alec Revell Band – the two men turned up to do battle over the gig. Arthur, backed by the Omega boys and a solic-itor, faced Don with the Alec Revell Band plus a few handpicked henchmen.

Despite the apparent prelude to a western-style ballroom brawl, the two men discussed the issue in a mature fashion. Chisnall said that he would agree to the Cy Laurie Club running the evening, but wondered if the Omega Band could be given the gig so at least he would be able to honour the contract he had made with them. Kingswell, thinking this sounded fair enough, agreed and sent Alec and his band off on another job. The wily Chisnall promptly called in a police sergeant as a precaution and called the Omega Band out on strike. Kingswell, left standing with a ballroom full of expectant punters but no band to entertain them, had no option but to admit defeat on that occasion and retire to lick his wounds. Kingswell laid claim to his rights to the lease on the grounds that the Cy Laurie Agency had already paid £700 towards renovation of the hotel, and ran an advertisement in the *Richmond and Twickenham Times* proclaiming the 'Grand Gala Opening Night' of the Cy Laurie Riverside Jazz Club on the evening of 9 February 1957.

The two camps spent the following week at loggerheads, growling at each other while attempting to come to an agreement for the following Saturday night. Signed a mere half-hour before the session began, the understanding was that Arthur Chisnall and the Eel Pie Jazz Club were granted the rights to

Fridays and Saturdays, but only until Easter. The Cy Laurie Agency was given the go-ahead to run sessions on other nights. Arthur, meanwhile, continued with his own canny form of combat, cryptically adding the letters 'E.S.O.B.R.M' to the bottom of the flyers he handed out. This apparently stood for 'Eel Pie Island Soldiers On – Beware Rumour-mongers', and was a direct reference to accusations made by Kingswell that Chisnall had started a whispering campaign around Twickenham, leading to poor attendance figures at sessions run by the Cy Laurie Agency.

In the midst of this mêlée, Michael Snapper finally succeeded in his quest to build a footbridge from Twickenham Embankment to Eel Pie Island, and the warring parties both took part in the celebratory opening ceremony in February 1957. It appears from newspaper reports that the Cy Laurie camp had their feet firmly under the table, as they got the gig inside the ballroom. It was also reported that they had signed a three-year contract with Snapper to run jive nights four evenings a week. Chisnall, they said, had organised 'a procession of jazz bands and a motley crew of Eelpiland Jazz Club members in fancy dress' to sing and dance their way from Twickenham Green to the bridge. The story of the joust over the jazz club goes quiet after this, and it would appear that Kingswell, faced with Arthur's doggedness, concluded that he might have bitten off more than he was able, or could be bothered, to chew, and he backed down.

According to the genial trumpet player Brian Rutland, Arthur was guilty of a bit of skulduggery himself. Brian had a band called the Grove Jazz Band (he lived in The Grove, Isleworth) which played regularly at the Barmy Arms pub opposite the island. Throughout 1955–56 they built up such a following that the pub was beginning to split at the seams and they decided to look for somewhere larger. Having got wind of Michael Snapper's recent renewal of the licence across the river, Brian arranged with him to use the ballroom free so long as the band brought a beer-buying crowd along with them. The Grove Jazz Band started to organise and play regular gigs on Eel Pie Island and enjoyed an increasingly successful run over a couple of months. Among the regulars in the crowd was Arthur Chisnall, whom Brian recalled as 'about 15 years older than most of us and obviously looking at the situation with an eye on the business side'. Remembering the night of the takeover, Brian said:

> One evening when I turned up with a few members of the band I was confronted by Arthur saying, 'I have come to an arrangement with Mr Snapper and will be running the sessions from now on. However, you can be a life-member.' He had even arranged for another band to play that evening without letting me know. I was gazumped! I was furious . . .

ABOVE: Snapper's bridge was opened by the Mayor of Twickenham on Saturday, 9 February 1957, with the Rowing Club, canoeists, two clergymen, sea-cadets and Cy Laurie's jazz band in attendance, followed by a reception at the hotel. The unusual concrete structure, by Gifford and Partners of Southampton, was held in place by two pre-tensioned cables anchored at each end and concealed in the beams supporting the deck. It was this neat concealment that proved the bridge's undoing, when sub-contractors for British Gas attached a gas pipe in 1987: the holes they drilled for the support brackets all but severed the cable inside one of the beams.

OPPOSITE: Brian Rutland, on trumpet, with The Grove Jazz Band at Eelpiland.

'I was gazumped! I was furious and after words were exchanged I left, swearing never to return' Brian Rutland of the Grove Jazz Band, victim of band 'gazumping' by Arthur Chisnall

LEFT: A young Mick Avory played one of his first gigs at Eel Pie Island in 1957, remembering it as the equivalent of 'playing Madison Square Garden'. Aged just 13, he was drummer with the First Molesey Skiffling Scouts ('We never went anywhere, we weren't a household name!'), booked as the support act for Bill Brunskill's Jazz Band. Mick went on to bigger and better things, drumming with one of the defining bands of the Sixties, The Kinks.

'**Since people were** determined to bounce as hard as they could on the floor, we would encourage them by telling them that the river was underneath. We said that the island was once in three parts and that one of the "joins" was under the hotel, and this would really get them going. They were determined to **go through it** and into the river!' *Arthur Chisnall*

Brian did not return to the island for many months, and then in a different capacity: 'I went there as a fellow club owner. My clubs in Feltham, Southall, Woking and Addlestone were also featuring some of the same leading jazz bands of that time.' An uneasy truce continued between the two men, but Rutland was 'too involved with other matters to hold a grudge against Arthur'.

Arthur had died by the time I talked to Brian, so I could not ask him for his side of this tale. But it has to be said that he never laid claim to being the sole founder of the jazz club; this was an accolade gradually bestowed upon him in the press by virtue of the social work for which he and the club became famous. Michael Snapper's son Emile said, 'It has always disappointed me that whenever you see write-ups about the club only Arthur Chisnall is mentioned. He was certainly a major catalyst and its front-man, but my father was key in setting it all up too.' Indeed, Michael Snapper even hired a dance instructor to come along and teach 'the Twickenham boys and girls some of the finer points of ballroom jive'.

THE FAMOUS BOUNCING FLOOR

Remembered by all for its sprung maple dance floor, built in the 1920s at the height of the fashion for tea-dances, the ballroom that had once witnessed graceful waltzes rapidly became the scene for swirling, twirling, jiving couples, as the dance styles imported via the American soldiers stationed in wartime Britain became all the rage. Virtually everyone I have spoken to recalls the floor with fondness, although not all believed that springs alone caused the bounce: the river was said to flow right under the ballroom. Club regular Gerry Loader told me: 'When the spring tides were around, it seemed that the dance floor was floating.' These stories appealed to Chisnall's sense of humour, and were perpetuated as a form of entertainment.

The rumours soon reached official ears and during one of the regular police inspections the superintendent pointed at the floor and asked, 'What's underneath that?' Arthur assured him that, despite the tales he might have heard, the floor was actually constructed on solid foundations, but it would be a shame to spoil the folklore, so would he mind keeping quiet about it?

The dance floor might have been a real talking point, but the rest of the hotel had obviously seen better days. Mike Peters recollects:

The building looked in danger of imminent collapse. The glorious arched window looking on to the Thames had lost most of its glass and I can well remember one winter evening, a blizzard blowing outside, seeing the wonderful Sandy Brown Band in overcoats, hats and gloves doing their best to entertain the dancers while snow drifted across the stage.

OPPOSITE: Background: the dilapidated ballroom. Top: Hawkwind founder Dave Brock on stage with Mike King, 1966. Bottom: Dave Brock dancing in the club.

'Full of dust and dilapidated, but we loved it. It was the greatest place to jive and there was no comparison with other venues' Mike & Triss Cole, who did much of their courting on the island in the late 1950s

'He was the most amazing guy, not a perfect one but an amazing one who changed so many of our young lives, often forever and for the better. All good salesmen know that the most powerful device they can implement to make a sale is to make the punters believe that they thought of the idea themselves. That's what Arthur did with Eel Pie Island: we thought it was our place that we had conjured up on our own and he was just someone who happened to be there, almost invisible, allowing us to be ourselves and grow from that. Of course, where Arthur differed from most salesmen was that there was nothing much in the way of material benefit in it for him, just the reflection of what it did for us. I just want people to know what a really **fantastic, influential and special** person he was'   *Karen O'Brien*

CHISNALL: BEARD & PIPE SMOKE

It was not music and dancing that had inspired Arthur to set up the club – his motives were entirely different. He had a keen interest in emerging youth culture, especially in the often extraneous ways the youth services of the day set out to accommodate it.

James Arthur White Chisnall was born on 3 June 1925 in Kingston-upon-Thames, to Elizabeth Goater Chisnall. The space for his father's details on his birth certificate was left blank. The man Elizabeth had expected to marry had returned from the First World War to an early grave thanks to mustard-gas poisoning; she continued to carry a torch for him, however, and named her only child after him. The young Arthur grew up devoid of a paternal relationship and had to work out for himself who his father might be. He remembered being sent to the local corner shop with an empty basket, a note and specific instructions from his mother: 'If the man is there give him the note. If the woman is there, buy a box of matches and come back.' Arthur continued: 'Having received the note, the man would regard me for a moment, ask for the basket, return it loaded and send me on my way. No money was ever requested.' The young boy sensed that this man was really his father, but nothing was ever confirmed to him.

Arthur and his mother lived with his grandparents, George and Rosella, who ran a shop. He adored his grandfather and the two were very close until he died

in November 1930 when Arthur was just five years old. His grandmother had died in January 1930, leaving him with just his mother, who struggled to keep the shop running for a year or two longer. In later life he described his grandmother as 'a cold woman at best. She did not like me and we avoided each other.' As he got older he realised that her dislike probably stemmed from the belief that he was responsible for ruining her daughter's life. Arthur commented: 'It was not really my fault. If I had been given the choice I would have arrived on the right side of the blanket, with a father, instead of the wrong side, without one. That choice, however, was not mine to make.'

Arthur described the departure of his grandfather from his life as 'a major trauma'. Many years later when he inherited his grandfather's chair he smashed it up, telling himself that he had no use for it. He went on to say: 'Later still, I realised I had not forgiven him for leaving me at a time when I felt vulnerable and alone.'

One can only speculate (especially as Arthur was incredibly adept about talking *around* the subject of himself) that it might have been this lack of a full family in his young life that spurred his passion, based on inherent empathy, for helping other young people who were struggling to find their place in society. His friend Jack Lambert commented: 'Eel Pie Island and the kids who went there – that was his

'It was great fun to be around when someone talked to Arthur about a problem. They went away thinking that he had solved it for them when in actual fact they had solved it for themselves! His genius was in his ability to get people to "join the dots". He was **like Socrates** – no answers, only questions – the greatest enabler I have ever known. A truly selfless man dedicated to others' *Jack Lambert*

'He played a unique and very important part not only in youth and music culture, but also in helping the very conservative world of the formal youth services come to grips with the issue of the "unclubbables"' *Peter Kuenstler*

'A wonderful human being who founded a generation of alternative thinkers and gave us joy, hope and a new future. The island was the original rave place – anything went, and we all reinvented ourselves from Mum and Dad's kids to wild new creatures. The world was our oyster and **the energy was atomic** – no need for drugs' *Simone Williams*

'His bedroom doubled as an information/research/direct action area. Heaped piles of newspapers everywhere to be stepped over, waiting to be sorted. Articles on young people, drugs, police and politicians to be cut out and filed. Apart from the perils underfoot, the room was in a stygian gloom, with a smell like ripe Camembert – Arthur was born without a sense of smell, stayed up most nights, slept by day and forgot to wash his socks! He was also **very good company** and, more than anything, he was always ready to listen and talk to anyone' *Auriol McKay*

'A practical revolutionary'
Tim Summers

'Often a parent will say, "I gave that boy everything." "Everything" in their terminology means material things. These are the parents who will insist on watching *Coronation Street* and won't discuss birth control with their children. [The teenagers] often come from comfortable backgrounds where they're given material things, but not the affection and, more importantly, the **understanding** they need'   *Arthur Chisnall*

ABOVE: Ken Colyer (on trumpet) and his band lead Chisnall (under the banner, with beard and glasses) and many of the Eelpiland club members on a CND march at Kings Cross Station, 1959.

family.' Arthur Chisnall was to display an exceptional talent and patience for understanding the problems faced by the young people around him, and an innovative ability to solve them.

Educated at a church school less than a hundred yards from his home, Arthur had struggled through his tuition, hampered by being forced to write with right-handed pens (he was left-handed) and being punished 'for spoiling charitably given church property' in his efforts. With no money to continue his formal education beyond the age of 14, he ventured out to get his first job – in the carpet department of a Kingston store, Hide & Co. This was clearly not what he felt he was destined for, but he lasted a few years until he volunteered for military service in 1942 and joined the Royal Engineers. Serving in a specialist communications unit in north Africa, he took part in Montgomery's 'Operation Bertram', which involved erecting dummy tanks in the south to throw Rommel off the scent of the army's true intentions. After the war, he worked on a community development programme in East Africa, before returning to England in 1951 to take a course in social science at Coleg Harlech in Wales. This helped to set him on the path that led to his Eel Pie Island role.

Arthur Chisnall's strengths lay in guiding and empowering others. This desire to facilitate was the real inspiration behind Eelpiland, the music scene being almost secondary. By and large, he viewed the musical acts he booked as the means of attracting the needful youngsters whom he wanted to reach out to and inspire. Although I heard him speak fondly of Ken Colyer, Cyril Davies and Jeff Beck, he certainly wasn't a passionate music fan. When I met Arthur in January 1996, I expected someone full of himself, a cool dude, a man-about-town. I was pleasantly surprised at his complete lack of over-inflated ego – and, I must admit, a little frustrated at his lack of tawdry tales of rock 'n' roll's finest. Here was a man who had booked the Rolling Stones, hung out with Rod Stewart, shared a beer with Eric Clapton, Jeff Beck and countless others, yet he preferred to talk about politics rather than partying, and was almost cross at my suggestion that he had seen a gap in the market for youth entertainment: 'No, no, you have to realise, I was a researcher, I was interested in why this generation of youngsters was different and how they could be helped. I wasn't looking at it commercially.'

In 1957, the Conservative Prime Minister Harold Macmillan famously declared: 'Most of our people have never had it so good.' After the austerity of wartime Britain, this statement would have rung true for many. In 1954 the last remnants of food rationing had been lifted, average wages were rising, employment levels were nearing full and Britain was experiencing a modest consumer boom. Labour-saving appliances – refrigerators, vacuum cleaners and washing machines – were owned by increasing

'We get everyone from professional workers to labourers. There are no social distinctions at all' Arthur Chisnall

'When you are young you look for the things that define "you" and when you find those things you feel like you've come home. That was just what it was like on the island – you felt as if you'd found **home**. Places such as the Crawdaddy and the Ricky Tick had some sort of credibility in their own way, but not anything close to the island'
Karen O'Brien

ABOVE RIGHT: A youthful Eric Clapton at L'Auberge coffee bar, a favourite pre-gig meeting-place just over Richmond Bridge.

numbers of households, and televisions were fast becoming the must-have source of entertainment. This was the era of 'keeping up with the Joneses'. Britain was officially an affluent society – particularly if you lived in the south.

Some teenagers, however, couldn't relate to this declaration of optimism. Certainly, they were experiencing an unprecedented economic freedom, and could lavish money on luxuries denied to their parents; they were presented with a burgeoning marketplace of youth-specific products such as clothes, records and magazines. But concurrent with this, the generation gap had widened to such an extent that many were feeling cut off from their elders and at odds with society.

In general, youth services in 1950s Britain were extremely conservative: a club leader in Huddersfield was dismissed in 1960 simply for allowing his charges to listen to rock and roll music and play darts. The county youth services thought it more appropriate that 'teenagers should be encouraged to take part in handicrafts and classical music'. This attitude was received with ridicule by the adolescents of the day; such 'opportunities' were completely irrelevant to their real needs. For the first time, young people were demanding space to evolve into themselves rather than merely replicate their parents. Arthur Chisnall was miles ahead of the game when it came to providing entertainment and understanding.

Alongside a venue for music and dancing, Eelpiland was for him first and foremost a vehicle for a 'social experiment' to reach out and help awkward groups of young people that were so perplexing to the authorities. Chisnall told me:

When I left college in 1950 I wanted to be involved with the community, but not in a position of authority. I wanted to observe and interact on a practical level.

This is exactly what he did at Eel Pie, describing the club as 'an open therapeutic community'.

By the turn of the decade the club had over 8,000 members representing a cosmopolitan cross-section. Arthur had created a club that covered two definitions of the word: on the one hand it was a social establishment but, very importantly, it also provided an alliance, a support group of like-minded people among whom members could feel at home.

Deliberately included among the members were professionals including a doctor, a psychologist and a policeman. Arthur actively sought to provide easy access for youngsters to people who could answer their questions in an informal environment on issues such as contraception or drugs. The club ran 'classes' on constructive skills including filling out job applications, writing CVs and interview techniques. The uptake of college places was actively promoted at a time when post-school education was not accessible to the majority.

'As the first person to go to Coleg Harlech from the island I owe everything to Arthur. One night, when I was standing next to him stamping wrists, he persuaded me to go – and then not only funded it, but drove me there too. Arthur told me Coleg Harlech would **change my life** – it did! I ended up as Assistant Principal at Bradford College, at the time the biggest in the country, and now, although retired, I edit a local newspaper in Spain, a journey started by Arthur, the most altruistic person I have ever met. The island taught me that life is too short: do it now, try it now, go for it. Arthur's philosophy represented the best of the Fifties and Sixties'   *Rod Sawyer*

Arthur had studied at Coleg Harlech in Wales, established in 1927 to provide learning opportunities for all adults, including those who, for whatever reason, had missed out when they were younger. He saw plenty of candidates at his club who had, as he put it, 'somehow or other been pushed off the ladder'. Through Eelpiland at least twenty young people were persuaded to take up study at Coleg Harlech and other institutions. Some were even funded by the club itself: gigs, dances and raffles were held specifically to raise money to send someone off to a new start. Arthur was also active in putting pressure on Middlesex County Council to give grants to students previously perceived by the authorities as 'no-hopers'.

Eelpiland members were also politically active: Arthur and other club members initiated involvement in movements such as CND and the Campaign Against Racial Discrimination. Political speakers often took to the stage and group discussions were encouraged. Arthur believed passionately in giving people information and allowing them to think for themselves.

EELPILAND, THE PRESS & PUBLIC PERCEPTION

Arthur's methods, which essentially involved listening to people and providing a nurturing, networking environment, were considered outlandish enough at the time to warrant a steady stream of press interest. Throughout much of the 1960s the Eel Pie Club was the subject of sometimes hostile and often bewildered coverage, written largely by patronising defenders of staid sensibilities. The tabloid consensus was that the club was a den of iniquity, a dubious devil's playground rife with sexual promiscuity and drugs.

A particularly denigratory but entirely predictable 1960 piece in the *Weekend Mail* was headed 'Down Among The Dead-Beats':

When the Saints Come Marching In, will they reek of oakum and armpits? Will they have hair like spun yarn, beards like spinach, and eyes like rissoles in the snow? . . . Any kind of clothing is worn, as long as it is crumpled and dirty; any kind of haircut as long as it is not cut at all; any kind of expression as long as it is expressionless.

This was illustrated with a set of 'shocking' photographs of people who, by today's standards, look as though they're merely having a bit of fun on an average Saturday night.

But the article had serious repercussions. Publication of photographs (without permission) allegedly led to two people losing their jobs. A row ensued between Associated Newspapers and the Eel Pie Club. Chisnall organised a petition asking for public representation on the Press Council, and the prob-

OPPOSITE: Arthur Chisnall (on the right) saw in Eelpiland a chance to test out his ideas on youth work. Thousands were to troop across the bridge, get their wrists stamped in lieu of tickets and enter his 'social experiment'.

'It was a notorious part of local folklore with a reputation for being a pretty lawless, drug-ridden place. Twickenham County schoolgirls had all been banned by our mothers from ever going there – so of course we all went! When you consider that my parents even banned the wearing of jeans, this constituted **a fair old rebellion'** *Judy Astley*

'I remember a young girl who had been given a clip round the ear for going to the island. She had, in fact, never been near the place, but seeing as she had already taken the punishment she thought she'd better come along and see what all the fuss was about' Arthur Chisnall

lems of press reporting were highlighted in a benefit gig. Labour MP Frank Allaun and Martin Ennals from the National Council for Civil Liberties spoke to the crowd, and Acker Bilk provided the entertainment. This event made the pages of *The Times Educational Supplement,* and the matter was subsequently brought up in a parliamentary debate by Frank Allaun. It led to the appointment of the first independent member to the Press Council, and a commitment to investigate press harassment of young people.

The inevitable result of these exaggerated shocker 'news' stories was only to add fuel to the fire that lured the young and prompted hellish fear in their parents. Virtually every youngster in the area was forbidden to go across that bridge. Author Judy Astley, then a Twickenham County schoolgirl, became a regular after being 'extremely jealous' as a 14-year-old 'when a group of fifth-formers went to see the Rolling Stones'. She had a letter published in the *Richmond and Twickenham Times* hitting out at criticisms of the club and the victimisation of youth:

> The standard of intelligence [at the club] is as high, if not higher, than that of many of those who do not check their facts before giving biased criticism about the behaviour of the younger generation.

She was justified: during research for a Schofield report on the sexual behaviour of young people, Peter Massey concluded that the island crowd were 'most articulate and enjoyable to talk with'.

In 1967, not long before Arthur Chisnall was forced to close the doors on Eelpiland, the Vicar of Twickenham publicly defended the club. Responding to a BBC television programme which had made allegations that came close to accusing Chisnall of encouraging drug use, under-age drinking and sexual promiscuity, the Rev. Derek Landreth spoke out in favour of Chisnall's work:

> It is the people who only hear about the goings-on at the island who kick up a fuss. Those who go and see it for themselves come away a lot happier. I think Mr Chisnall is helping in quite a unique way because he is providing a very large community into which young people who are 'out' can come in. The youngsters are extremely coherent and the fact that Chisnall has no formal qualifications and is a solo worker is almost certainly key to his success. I have no criticisms of the island. Arthur Chisnall is one of the few people, if not the only person in the country, who has really got to grips with the situation.

No one could pretend that there was no sexual misbehaviour – we are talking, after all, about a gathering of hundreds of hormonally charged teenagers – but it was hardly the bacchanalian lust-fest envisaged by fretful parents. The extent of the alleged brazen

HIGH MINDS and LOW HEELS

Stomping with the eggheads
on Eel Pie Island

A "TRAD" jazz band blared out the music for 300 pairs of dancing feet. And I stood at the entrance to the dance-hall on Eel Pie Island, in the middle of the Thames at Twickenham, using a rubber stamp on the wrists of still more dancers surging to get in.

"You must realise that what goes on in this place is the expression of the latent desire among the young to get away from mass media and regimentation," said the organiser, Arthur Chisnell, an antique dealer.

"Then what am I stamp-ing their wrists for?" I asked. "Is it a way of count-ing your four and six-pences?" For as I stamped, Arthur took the lolly.

Actually, the reason for the cattle-like branding was to ensure that the dancers could leave and return to the hall again without hav-ing to pay more. Frankly, I liked the job. Eel Pie jazz girls are pretty.

The Eel Pie Island club was celebrating its fifth anniversary. Its members were unusual for such a place. Budding architects, accountants, doctors, engin-eers, students of every description solemnly held out their hands for my stamp.

Any moment now Mr. John Stonehouse, Labour M.P. for Wednesbury, Staffs. was due. He was going to talk about Africa. Mr. Gresham Cooke, Tory M.P. for Twickenham, has attended.

ENTHUSIASM

Here was a side of the jazz cult not generally known. From among these prancing, spinning figures came many of the youngsters who puzzled their elders with their enthusiasm for the Ban the Bomb marches and the anti-Apartheid demon-strations. They all seemed highly intelligent.

Yet on the face of it I seen this sort of thing There were the

swinging till the sweat made their hair wet. There were the courting couples on the grass by the river.

But, in fact, it was totally different from other places.

Mr. Chisnell ran his hands through long grey hair that belied his mere 36 years and explained: "This place started as a jazz club. Now it's one of the biggest political discussion centres in this part of Greater London There are 8,386 members.

"The bands play only on Saturdays and Sundays. During the week members jam the bar and keep the juke box going while dis-cussing all sorts of serious topics.

"We have direct connec-tions with the Campaign for Nuclear Disarmament, the Anti-Apartheid League, and the National Council for Civil Liberties.

"But we're not tied down to any one line of political thought."

A young B.O.A.C. employee nodded. "I used to be a Mau Mau fighter," he said.

Some of the couples courted and married from this club, like 19-year-old Terry Linehan, of Acton, and his wife. Jeanette. "When we're able to get a baby sitter we still come," said Terry. "It doesn't mat-ter if you wear a suit, like me, or a sloppy-joe and a funny hat. We're all friends here."

Said June Lawson, trainee fashion designer, of North Wembley: "We're rebels. My parents are Conserva-tive. But I think we all differ from our parents. That's why I've been in Ban the Bomb marches and things like that."

PINTS

An estate agent downed a pint of beer and gravely handed a pint of cider to his fiancee. On Eel Pie Island most of the girls drink pints.

"You can see how my original jazz club has grown into something far bigger," said Mr. Chisnell. "We're not troubled by hooligan gangs. The hooligans tried to take the club over once or twice, but from the day I opened I've worked closely with the police.

"Of course, when some guest bands come they bring their own followers

Colin Govet, aged 18, and his wife of only three weeks, 16-year-old Barbara. They describe them-selves as "folk musicians"

and some of these get lively But we calm them down."

Eel Pie Island has some delightful riverside houses. What do these residents think of the noisy club gatherings?

I found some of them in the club bar. Said one: "When the club first opened we had grave doubts. Now a lot of us are members. We don't dance of course. We're far too old for that lark."

A young man in jeans and a brilliantly-coloured vest clasped a beautiful young brunette round the waist. "Get this straight," he said, "during the week I wear pin-striped pants. I'm a City bloke. But this is the best way I know of getting away from it all."

As, promptly at 11 o'clock, the youngsters streamed home over the bridge to the "mainland" I thought I knew what the "City bloke" meant

Peter Earle

THANK YOU!   PLEASE COME AGAIN

Over the bridge to the "mainland"

ABOVE: This 'News of the World' article of 1961 showed considerable sympathy for the social and political aspects of Chisnall's work on Eel Pie Island.

HOUSE KEYS

MOBILE PHONE

PIPE
MATCHES
TOBACCO

WALLET

SONG SHEET

CONDOMS

SPECTACLES

'**Sex and drugs and rock 'n' roll**: well, we had the sex and the rock 'n' roll, but there wasn't much in the way of drugs. We went there for the music and the kinfolk. There weren't any punch-ups or fights, just a fantastic bonding . . . There were **lots and lots of girls**, and you had to dance, because the sprung floor in the ballroom went up and down like a **trampoline**'

Trevor Baylis

'A lot of people weren't allowed to go to the island. Their parents forbade it, which was ironic really because you were so safe there' Karen O'Brien

behaviour varies greatly, depending on who you talk to – some recall 'orgies' while others were lucky to get an innocent snog. As for drugs, it was the 1960s, but for many people they simply were not on the menu, and very few could afford them. Newcastle Brown was the most intoxicating substance likely to get into the bloodstream of the majority of island club-goers.

The island's most famous resident of today, Trevor Baylis, inventor of the clockwork radio and himself the host of many a legendary shindig, told me about his early experiences. 'Was it really debauched over there, Trevor?' I asked. He laughed.

Well, it depends on what you mean by debauched. When you were 16 or 17, sex was very much on the horizon – all you could think about was the girl next door! You know, all the girls were scantily dressed and we blokes were, well, very horny! So we were just having a lot of fun, a few drinks, some dancing and shagging ourselves silly . . .

Vivacious raconteurs such as Trevor Baylis and George Melly seemed to 'get a lot' on Eel Pie, but in general the scene surely was not very different from that for subsequent teenagers – a minority were actually having sex; most were just talking about it. What made behaviour at Eelpiland scandalous at the time was probably the fact that these youngsters were so much freer in their self-expression than the prevailing norms. So what if you romped around outside on the grass? So what if a bloke put his hand up your top? So what if someone saw you? This unconventional conduct and defiance of perceived public morals shocked and outraged the older generation, raised as they had been on the tail-end of Victorian hypocrisy and keep-it-behind-closed-doors values. Licentious legends may have been the talk of the town, but most people, particularly girls, who went to the island remember how secure they felt. A few parents were even in favour. Summing up the attitude of those most opposed to Eelpiland, Arthur Chisnall said: 'Our main "crime" was to teach people to think for themselves – an unforgivable sin!'

Despite coming across much bafflement and umbrage among the 'establishment', Chisnall also found allies for his cause. The work he was carrying out on Eel Pie Island was looked at with interest by figures in authority. He had connections with Leslie Wilkins in the Home Office, Peter Kuenstler at the United Nations and many educational institutions abroad. Eelpiland was used as a model for similar projects in Berlin. At least two films were made at the club, one of them a *Look at Life* feature for Granada TV called 'Who needs Eel Pie?' and another made by a German film crew.

My friendship with Arthur developed in the last

OPPOSITE: Trevor Baylis today, still going strong in his seventies, with his trusty friend Ike and his uncompleted, home-made Mercedes. Inset: Trevor's reminders for going out, pinned to his door.

twelve years of his life. He quickly became a good friend, and I always enjoyed going round to see him. His kitchen table was forever piled high with paperwork and he invariably had something interesting to say about current politics. He remained an eternal networker, continually endeavouring to forge links between people that might benefit them. I never left his house empty-handed: an ornament, a plant cutting, a book or some other bit of paraphernalia would be presented on my exit. I was never entirely sure if he was extremely generous or just saving himself a trip to the charity shop – I suspect it was a bit of both! As others have said of him, he taught me things without my realising it, and I am delighted to have known him.

'MAY THE FORCE BE WITH YOU'

Despite the common belief that Eelpiland was a vice-den run by Satan himself, there was very little crime there. As a 25-year-old police officer, Eddie Searle worked a plain-clothes shift there every weekend in the early 1960s. He remembers the first time, in 1961, and his enthusiasm for the prospects on offer: 'ample scope to find work and customers for the charge room'. He admits he shared the view of many of his colleagues that 'Arthur must have been a shrewd operator who was making more than a fair living from the "weirdy beardies", or "great un-washed" as they were commonly known locally', and

he was wholly unaware of the benevolent activities behind the scenes.

To his surprise, Arthur invited him in and offered him complete freedom to wander anywhere.

I moved around the dance hall, trying to be as inconspicuous as possible, looking carefully and listening hard. Where was all the crime I was so sure must be abounding? Eaves-dropping at various groups gave me snatches of conversation about the atomic bomb, art, the quality of the music and the beer, the merits of this or that girl, further education, but nothing that interested me as a policeman.

Repeating his island beat on the following two weekends, he again trudged back across the bridge 'empty-handed and beginning to doubt my ability as a police officer. It certainly opened my eyes to another view of the world,' he remarked. His initial prejudice fell away, and he found that he was becoming interested in the club and those who frequented it.

I could not see how there were so many people closely confined without there being fights or similar trouble; it was remarkable.

Arthur had potential troublemakers under control. He once told me how small gangs of Teddy Boys would saunter over looking for a scrap.

We noticed that they would come in, drink their first pint, buy a second and then start

ABOVE LEFT: *The famous mural behind the stage, artist unknown.*

ABOVE: The Crane River Jazz Band were key players in the south London skiffle boom, which inspired many to pick up an instrument and just play. The skiffle movement provided a fundamental impetus for the British Blues boom of the Sixties.

looking for trouble. So, just before they ordered their second beer we would get on the phone to the police who would obligingly come over and shepherd them off the island. It took the Teddy Boys some time to cotton on to what we were up to, but eventually we were off their list of calling places.

And members so valued their club and their involvement in it that they themselves provided 'a tacit wall of resistance to any rowdies who might drift in'.

Virtually everyone I have interviewed remarked on the fact that there was never any trouble on the island. The few crimes Eddie Searle recalls were only indirectly related to the club: thieves took advantage of people being across the river to break into cars parked on the Embankment.

SKIFFLE, ELECTRIC GUITARS & THE BRITISH BLUES

Around the time that London was starting to swing into the Sixties a new type of music was making itself heard. Fuelled by the inspirational anyone-can-have-a-go nature of skiffle, and the increasing availability of imported recordings from across the Atlantic, a new generation of Brits played their own version of rock 'n' roll. Most relevant to our story, they began to sow the seeds of a home-grown version of the blues.

Evolving in turn-of-the-century America, skiffle was initially played to raise rent money, the word being slang for 'rent party'. Tunes were improvised on anything from tea chests, saws and washboards to more traditional jazz instruments. The sound underwent a revival in spirit around 1949 when, just a few miles down the road from Eel Pie Island, the Crane River Jazz Band (including Ken Colyer, Monty Sunshine, Sonny Morris and Lonnie Donegan), began to hone their art in a hut at the side of the White Hart pub on Bath Road.

By the time the Eel Pie Club was up and running, skiffle music was generally what filled the gap while the headline band took a break (PA systems and DJs were novelties in those days). Also known as 'breakdown groups', the performers would be a mix of whoever felt like playing, the instruments would be an assortment of whatever happened to be handy and the sound was an amalgamation of jazz, blues, gospel, whatever took their fancy. Gradually skiffle took on a life of its own, becoming nationally recognised when Lonnie Donegan hit the top ten with *Rock Island Line* at the beginning of 1956.

Donegan inspired a new generation and reclaimed music for the masses. The notion that you had to be educated and wear a nice white suit to play in a band was kicked out of the door; music-making was suddenly there for everyone who wanted to have a go. Skiffle became the bridge between jazz, rock 'n' roll and the blues. All over south-west London and beyond, young lads were inspired to pick up guitars

'Cyril was a real supernova. A musical prodigy, he sang, played banjo, guitar and harmonica. Fellow musicians called him a musical genius with a purist's vision' Todd Allen

'**Cyril Davies** was the first person I saw there. The thrill of being able to see a great band every week was so exciting. My whole life changed. It was beer, blues and birds! I was at Twickenham Art School at the time and we'd invariably have our end-of-term dances at Eel Pie Island. I even booked the Stones for one and had my band, the Muleskinners, open for them. I also remember Long John Baldry coming over to me one night in the bar. Towering over me, he put his finger on my head and said, "Hello Mac, would you like a drink?" Well, that was a big moment for me, having my friends see that **I knew John!**'

Ian McLagan (right), keyboardist with the Small Faces

OPPOSITE: Cyril Davies, an unsung hero in the British Blues explosion. John Adams: 'I met Cyril, Rod Stewart and Long John Baldry on a number of occasions, I think some time between 1963 and 1964 when I was playing with Tony "Duster" Bennett. Although we went to other clubs, it was Eel Pie Island that really won our allegiance and where we all got our inspiration.'

ABOVE RIGHT: Ian McLagan now lives in the US and plays with the Bump Band.

and make their way towards the stage at Eel Pie Island.

In the mid 1950s a pair of musicians who had been doing the rounds in various jazz bands were drawn together through a shared passion for American blues. Alexis Korner and Cyril Davies, generally known as the daddies of British R 'n' B, were instrumental in turning young Brits on to the blues. Forming Blues Incorporated in 1961, noteworthy among other things for being the first amplified R 'n' B group in the country, Davies and Korner embraced many a budding young musician – such as Long John Baldry, Charlie Watts, Paul Jones and Art Wood – within the fluid line-up of the band. Chisnall, with his knack for picking up on new trends, booked Davies and Korner to bring their thumping new sounds to rock the crowd at Eel Pie Island.

After musical differences pushed the pair apart – Korner was once more veering towards jazz, whereas Davies was uncompromising in his pursuit of the Chicago blues sound – the Cyril Davies All Stars was formed, fronted by the towering Baldry and also featuring drummer Carlo Little, Jeff Beck and, for a short while, future Led Zeppelin co-founder Jimmy Page. The band, with varying line-ups, played at Eel Pie until Cyril's untimely death on 7 January 1964. Arthur Chisnall said of Davies:

He'd nurtured R 'n' B through a period when you couldn't earn your dinner with it, let alone

make a living. Just at the time when he should have made a bomb, should have been 'the man', he got pleurisy and died.

Like Colyer, Davies is an unsung hero of the British musical heritage, who lit the fuse to a revolution whose influence is still apparent today.

After his death, Long John Baldry took the helm, honouring a booking at Eel Pie Island the very day that his mentor died. The Cyril Davies All Stars were renamed the Hoochie-Coochie Men. Featuring a blistering line-up that included Rod Stewart, they thrilled thousands at their frequent island gigs. The London art colleges provided a steady stream of inspired meetings of musical minds and an audience eager for the new grooves, and the Eel Pie Hotel became a veritable hot-house of home-grown talent. Chisnall's open-minded approach allowed for a freedom relished by performers and audiences alike. With Muddy Waters, B. B. King and Howlin' Wolf ringing in their ears, today's global superstars hauled their drum-kits, guitars, huge Hammond organs, amps and enthusiasm across that narrow bridge to the stage. The hotel itself may have been crumbling but inside a fresh creativity was being born; the musical world was to be changed forever.

A veritable *Who's Who* of musical names graced the stage at the Eel Pie Island Hotel throughout the eleven years that Chisnall was at its helm. It was nothing out of the ordinary in those days to hang out

'Cyril Davies with his Rhythm 'n' Blues All Stars played as though their lives depended on it, Cyril standing at the side of the stage blowing like **a whirlwind**. I was hooked. Every Sunday, he introduced me to visiting American musicians – Howlin' Wolf, Sonny Boy Williamson, Hubert Sumlin – and, of course, his very own singer, Long John Baldry. I still maintain that one of Baldry's subsequent bands, Steampacket, is the best live ensemble I've ever seen and heard'   *Ian Hamilton*

at the bar between sets with Rod Stewart, Long John Baldry, Ronnie Wood, Mick Jagger, Jeff Beck, John Mayall or Eric Clapton, all taking their first steps on the road to stardom. 'They'd all just come and go as ordinary people,' said Chisnall. Friendships at the art schools – Ealing, Kingston, Harrow, Twickenham – created an almost incestuous network of bands, with musicians shifting between transient line-ups: Blues Incorporated, the Artwoods, the Faces, Cream, the Yardbirds, Steampacket, the Tridents and the Rolling Stones.

Mike Elliott, who was given a room at the hotel in 1962–63 in return for working at the bar, remembers seeing a fresh-faced, nervous-looking Rod Stewart waiting in the wings for Long John Baldry to finish so he could go on. After an island gig one night, Baldry came across Stewart playing harmonica in the fog at Twickenham Station, and asked him if he wanted to join his band.

Long John Baldry, back in England in September 2000, went to visit Arthur Chisnall. Arthur and I took him on a trip down memory lane over the bridge to Eel Pie, while along the way John talked with great fondness about the fantastic times he had playing at the hotel. He boomed:

> There was simply nowhere else like it. My career really began on this little island. Arthur was something special, he nurtured both the musicians and the audiences who came to

watch us. I met, and played with, some of the best here, the cream of the crop of fantastic musicians. The venue was legendary long before it had even closed down.

One regular band was the Artwoods, who effectively had a residency there. For Art Wood the place held special memories, not least the fact that his brothers Ted and Ronnie played there too. He claimed his band held the attendance record, beating the now so much more famous Stones. 'It was always packed but there was never any trouble, just a wonderful atmosphere.' He often told a story about the inconvenience of needing to use the loo while playing:

> The toilets were right at the back of the hall and as it was so packed it was much easier to use a bottle in the dressing room above the stage. Well, sometimes the bottle would get knocked over and it would all drip through the floorboards on to the band. Not a very nice story, but true!

Ron Wood also tells this story, but in his version the contents of the bottle are his and they end up dripping down upon his brother and his band. There is no reason to doubt either of them . . . According to the Artwoods guitarist, Derek Griffiths:

> It was just so special. Other gigs were just gigs, but the island was something else. We took an almost corporate pride in playing there. You'd

ABOVE: Long John Baldry and Arthur Chisnall revisit Eel Pie Island in 2000.

OPPOSITE TOP LEFT: Steampacket: Long John Baldry and Rod Stewart on vocals, Brian Auger on the Hammond organ and Julie Driscoll on female vocals. Auger recalled Baldry as a great cartoonist who would draw caricatures of them on the band room walls: 'Every time we returned to play at Eel Pie Island, I noticed that we were all becoming more and more like our caricatures, which I found rather scary . . .'

OPPOSITE TOP RIGHT: Long John Baldry singing at Eel Pie Island.

OPPOSITE RIGHT: The Artwoods (left to right): Malcolm Pool, Art Wood, Keef Hartley, Derek Griffiths and Jon Lord.

OPPOSITE: Original Eel Pie contracts for Steampacket and the Artwoods.

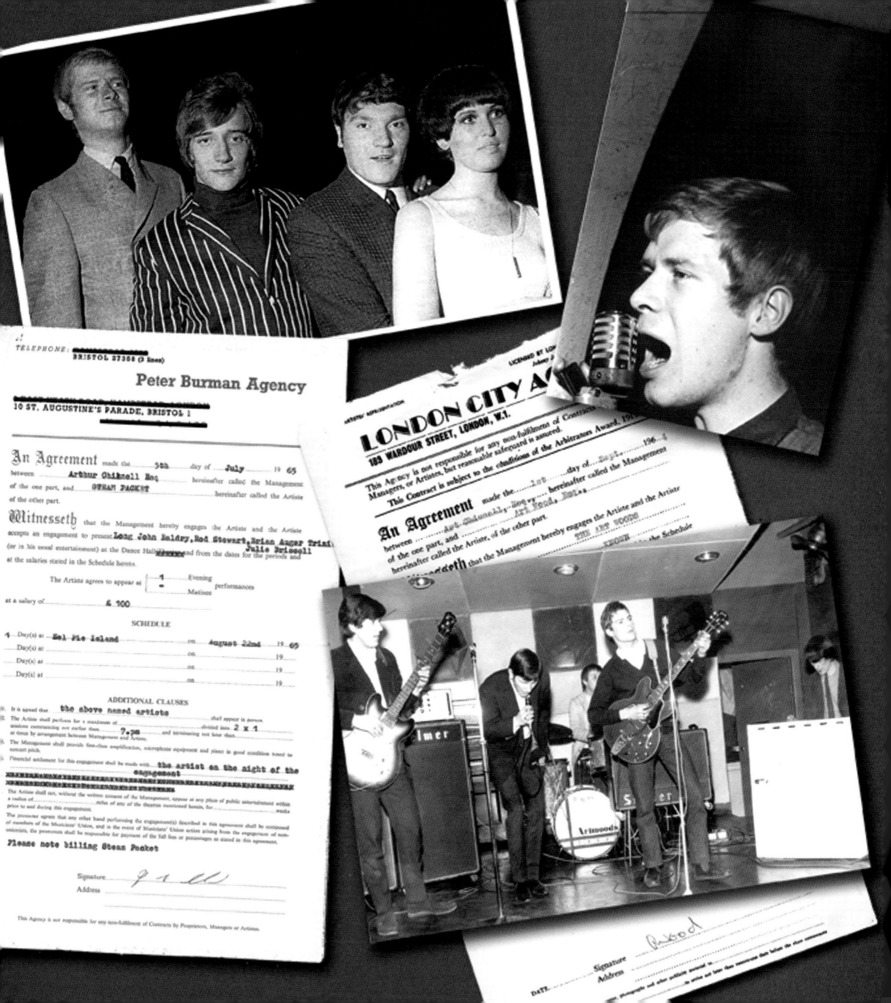

TELEPHONE: BRISTOL 27358 (3 lines)

Peter Burman Agency

10 ST. AUGUSTINE'S PARADE, BRISTOL 1

An Agreement made the **5th** day of **July** 19 **65**
between **Arthur Chisnell Esq** hereinafter called the Management
of the one part, and **STEAM PACKET**
of the other part, hereinafter called the Artiste

Witnesseth that the Management hereby engages the Artiste and the Artiste
accepts an engagement to present **Long John Baldry, Rod Stewart, Brian Auger Trinity**
(or in his usual entertainment) at the Dance Hall/Theatre and from the dates for the periods and **Julie Driscoll**
at the salaries stated in the Schedule hereto.

The Artiste agrees to appear at ☒ 1 Evening performances
Matinee

at a salary of .... £ 100

SCHEDULE

Day(s) at **Eel Pie Island**	on **August 22nd** 19 **65**
Day(s) at	on 19
Day(s) at	on 19
Day(s) at	on 19

ADDITIONAL CLAUSES

It is agreed that **the above named artists**

The Artiste shall perform for a minimum of .... shall appear in person.
sessions commencing not earlier than **7.pm** divided into **2 x 1**
at times by arrangement between Management and Artiste.

The Management shall provide first-class amplification, microphone equipment and piano in good condition tuned to concert pitch.

Financial settlement for this engagement shall be made with **the artist on the night of the engagement**

The Artiste shall not, without the written consent of the Management, appear at any place of public entertainment within a radius of .... miles of any of the theatres mentioned herein, for .... weeks prior to and during this engagement.

The promoter agrees that any other band performing the engagement(s) described in this agreement shall be composed of members of the Musicians' Union, and in the event of Musicians' Union action arising from the engagement of non-unionists, the promoter shall be responsible for payment of the full fees or percentages as stated in this agreement.

Please note billing Steam Packet

Signature ....
Address ....

This Agency is not responsible for any non-fulfilment of Contracts by Proprietors, Managers or Artistes.

LICENSED BY LO..

LONDON CITY A

189 WARDOUR STREET, LONDON, W.1.

This Agency is not responsible for any non-fulfilment of Contracts
Managers, or Artistes, but reasonable safeguard is assured.

This Contract is subject to the conditions of the Arbitrators Award, 19...

An Agreement made the .... day of ....Sept... 196...
between .... hereinafter called the Management
of the one part, and .... ART ROOD, Notts.
of the other part, hereinafter called the Artiste .... **THE ART WOODS**

Witnesseth that the Management hereby engages the Artiste and the Artiste .... **FROM** .... the Schedule

Signature .... Rwood
DATE ....
Address ....

'I went to this venue when I was 14 when it was a jazz club on a Saturday night in the haunted ballroom. When the sprung floor still worked, **footprints on the ceiling** from an earlier age. My dad, who grew up in Twickenham, was reputed to have sung in this hallowed hall as a youth preparing to go to war' *Martin*

OPPOSITE: It was the tradition to hold musicians upside-down and get them to stamp their painted feet on the ballroom ceiling.

ABOVE: The Velvelettes lend their backing vocals to Long John Baldry.

OVERLEAF: Background: Grace Marrs, who ran the bar with her husband Jack. Top left: An unidentified singer gives it his all. Centre: Bill for repairs to the dance floor. Right: Girls dancing on the not-so-clean floor!

Pages 72–73: The Rolling Stones played fourteen gigs in 1963 to huge crowds.

look out from the stage and that sprung floor would be rockin'. People would not just be piggy-backing, but double piggy-backing. It couldn't happen today – Health and Safety would close it down; but it did happen and thank God it did. We're poorer for the fact that we'll never have another Eel Pie Island. I wish I could take my kids there – they'd love it. Art [Chisnall] was much more than just a promoter to us. We had to deal with some pretty hard, almost gangster-like promoters who'd drag you into the bar if it had been a good night or have a go at you if it hadn't. Well, Art was very different – a very avuncular, kind person, and there was never any nonsense about the money, it was always there at the end of the gig. The island was a sea of seemingly anti-establishment bohemians, but actually it was very, very safe there and bloody great!

'I started to go there for the jazz, and remember that floor. What we'd do was stand in the middle and it would bounce up and down so much, you didn't even have to dance, it would go at least **six or seven inches** up in the air. When I was a beatnik back in the early Sixties that was the only thing there was really. You'd go to Richmond and sit around in a coffee bar [L'Auberge] on a Saturday afternoon, just waiting till it was time to go over the bridge to the island to see all these great bands, like Ken Colyer; and then of course it changed to R 'n' B and you'd see the Stones there. It was a fantastic place; but I do remember the trouble we had trying to haul John Mayall's Hammond organ across that bridge!' *Eric Clapton*

INVOICE

R & M (Construction) Co.

BUILDERS & DECORATORS

153. HARLINGTON ROAD
HILLINGDON,
MIDDX.

Tel; UX 34134

A.Chisnall Esq.,
13,Spencer Road,
TWICKENHAM,
Middx.

11th November 61

Repairs to dance floor at
Eel Pie Island Twickenham

to the taking up of the
existing floor and re-
laying with Jap Maple
T&g,using the secret nailed
method of fixing.Total
area 80 sq.feet   23 12 0

                  TOTAL £23 12 0

PAID WITH THANKS.
DATE 13 November 1961   NETT
R. & M. (CONSTRUCTION) CO.

The Rolling Stones play Eel Pie, 1963: 'Never mind the hotel, the bloody island was overflowing. The hall was solid, the grounds were solid and there were queues back over the bridge; it was hair-raising really. In theory we should have stopped the music and told everyone to leave, but we would have been torn to pieces if we had; there'd have been a riot!' Arthur Chisnall

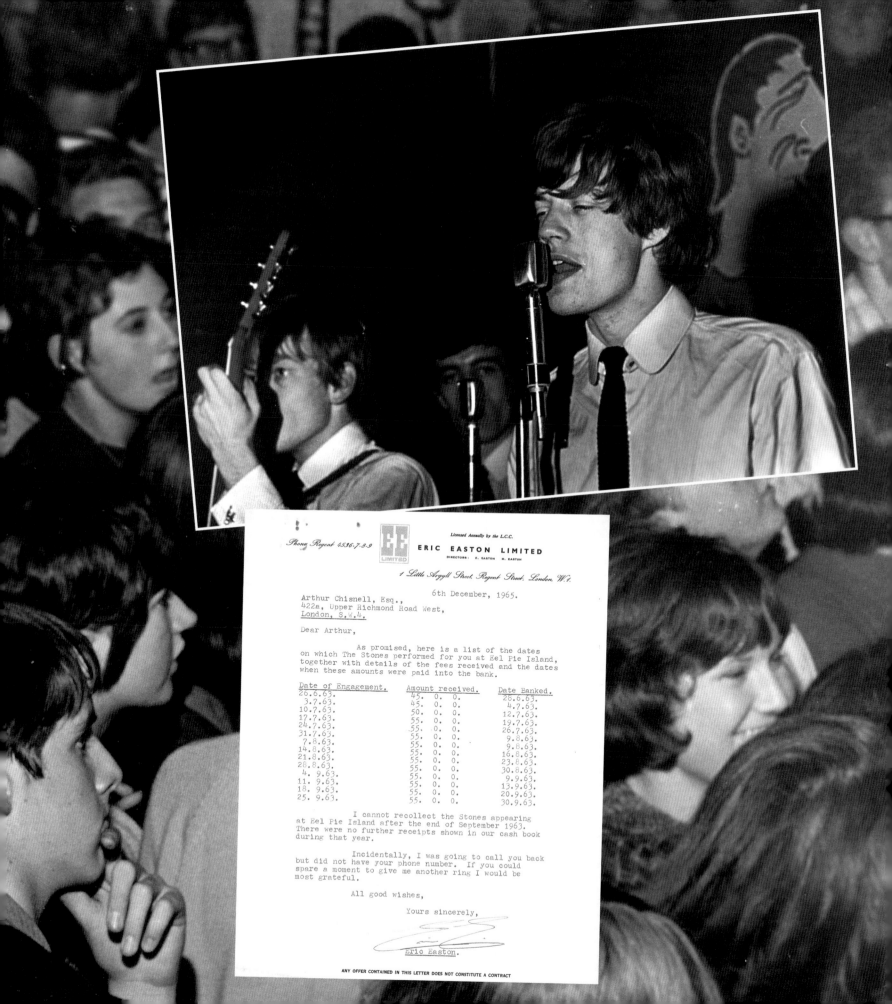

Phone Regent 4536·7·8·9

ERIC EASTON LIMITED

Licensed Annually by the L.C.C.

DIRECTORS: E. EASTON   M. EASTON

1 Little Argyll Street, Regent Street, London, W.1.

6th December, 1965.

Arthur Chisnell, Esq.,
422a, Upper Richmond Road West,
London, S.W.4.

Dear Arthur,

As promised, here is a list of the dates on which The Stones performed for you at Eel Pie Island, together with details of the fees received and the dates when these amounts were paid into the bank.

Date of Engagement.	Amount received.	Date Banked.
26.6.63.	45. 0. 0.	28.6.63.
3.7.63.	45. 0. 0.	4.7.63.
10.7.63.	50. 0. 0.	12.7.63.
17.7.63.	55. 0. 0.	19.7.63.
24.7.63.	55. 0. 0.	26.7.63.
31.7.63.	55. 0. 0.	9.8.63.
7.8.63.	55. 0. 0.	9.8.63.
14.8.63.	55. 0. 0.	16.8.63.
21.8.63.	55. 0. 0.	23.8.63.
28.8.63.	55. 0. 0.	30.8.63.
4. 9.63.	55. 0. 0.	9.9.63.
11. 9.63.	55. 0. 0.	13.9.63.
18. 9.63.	55. 0. 0.	20.9.63.
25. 9.63.	55. 0. 0.	30.9.63.

I cannot recollect the Stones appearing at Eel Pie Island after the end of September 1963. There were no further receipts shown in our cash book during that year.

Incidentally, I was going to call you back but did not have your phone number. If you could spare a moment to give me another ring I would be most grateful.

All good wishes,

Yours sincerely,

Eric Easton.

ANY OFFER CONTAINED IN THIS LETTER DOES NOT CONSTITUTE A CONTRACT

The Rolling Stones played a total of fourteen dates on the island, from 26 June to 25 September 1963, starting on a fee of £45 and finishing on £55. Brian Jones had called Arthur to ask if the Stones could play at the club, conscious of the fact that they were original island members and knowing that the group was getting so big that it would soon be impossible. Arthur recalled:

> If we'd realised just how big they had got we would have cancelled it . . . Thankfully the crowd were cool, they weren't screaming hysterically like a Beatles crowd would have been; they were there for the music. We had no option other than to let them get on with it, but, boy, it was a neurotic few hours.

Under the moniker of Davie Jones and the Manish Boys, a 17-year-old took to the island stage half a dozen times in 1964, playing a support slot to Long John Baldry and Alex Harvey. He went on to change his name and become the super-star David Bowie.

On his 1973 *Pin-Ups* album, Bowie listed Eel Pie Island among his favourite haunts.

The list of great names goes on, featuring not just those associated with the British R 'n' B explosion but also some of their inspirational gurus, such as Buddy Guy, who played the island with Rod Stewart and the Soul Agents on his first visit to Britain in 1965; Memphis Slim, John Lee Hooker, Jessie Fuller and Champion Jack Dupree. Reggae supremo Jimmy Cliff had half a dozen dates in the summer of 1966 and, paving yet another innovative musical way with their psychedelic sounds, Pink Floyd played for a fee of £75 in March, and then £100 in July, of 1967. British folk exponents Fairport Convention took to the stage for one of their earliest gigs the following month.

The Who are often mentioned in the same breath as the Rolling Stones when it comes to the history of Eel Pie Island. This has always puzzled me, because Arthur Chisnall was adamant that he never booked them: 'We really didn't want all those Mods haring

ABOVE: A German film crew records events.

OPPOSITE: The back sleeve of David Bowie's LP of favourite songs, 'Pin-Ups'.

'**Eel Pie was outrageous** and very attractive to me. It had this long bar with lots of places to lean on and I drank lots of Guinness there and met lots of blokes who thought I was older than I was. I really loved the beatnik feel of the place. It was languid, **romantic** and **sexy**, and at the same time had this quality of a seedy, rundown Roman villa. It seemed totally forbidden, which is what made it attractive. The main room was huge and I would hear stories about there being a backstage room with a bed where the musicians would take anyone who wanted to go! I remember paying four pennies to cross the bridge! And sometimes we didn't have the four pennies, and would run across quick before they could catch us!'
Caroline Margery Dunn

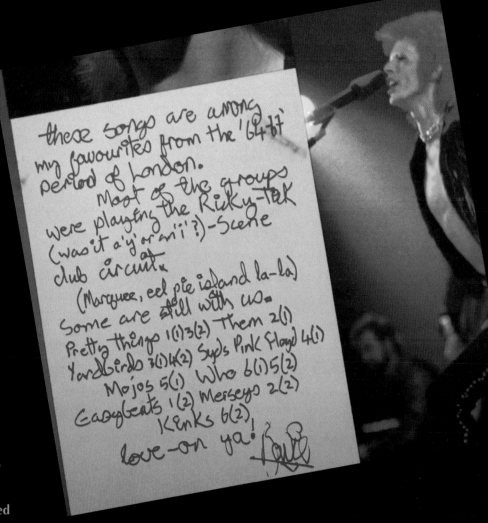

these songs are among my favourites from the '64+67' period of London.
Most of the groups were playing the Ricky-Tick (was it a'y'or an'i'?)–Scene club circuit.
(Marquee, eel pie island la-la) Some are still with us.
Pretty things 1(1)3(2) Them 2(1)
Yardbirds 3(1)4(2) Syd's Pink Floyd 4(1)
Mojos 5(1) Who 6(1)5(2)
Easybeats 1(2) Merseys 2(2)
Kinks 6(2)
love-on ya!

'**I'd bought a Daimler Limousine** from a neighbour who needed a quick sale. I offered him a pound note and he took it! It ended up in the car park behind Church Street awaiting repairs, but was a **great crash pad** if you missed the last bus home. Word got around and countless people would come up to me at the island on a Saturday night to ask for the key (which always got returned on the Sunday). I lent it out one Saturday and the next day the chap came up to me and said, "Jack, you bastard, you took the car away." Well, I hadn't, but I think the council had treated it as abandoned and taken it.

'About nine months later two girls came into L'Auberge in Richmond asking for me. They were from Dallas, Texas, and had been told that when they visited London they hadn't seen the sights if they hadn't been to the island and spent the night in Jack's limo!' *Jack Lambert*

'**The island** was the weekly pilgrimage to experience Newcastle Brown and Jessie Fuller singing 'San Francisco Bay Blues', Cyril Davies playing 'Country Line Special', Rod the Mod Stewart singing (and dancing!) 'Bye Bye Blackbird' with Long John Baldry, Alex Harvey wowing the women with his **pelvic thrusts** and Jeff Beck in the Tridents playing guitar with his back to the audience. Oh yeah, and the Stones and Artwoods' *Neil Bryson*

OPPOSITE: The battered ballroom of the Eel Pie Island Hotel.

RIGHT: Looking out from the club cloakroom.

across the bridge on scooters.' The mystery was solved when Pete Townshend told me that they did play there – but only once, in 1968, after the Chisnall era. So many people count them among their Eel Pie memories that it must have been a pretty packed night – or, more likely, they are one of the names to *say* you saw.

ALL GOOD THINGS COME TO AN END

Eelpiland was forced to close its doors on 4 September 1967, after eleven fantastic years in which a total of 30,000 members had enjoyed some of the best and most innovative musical entertainment Britain had to offer – and countless hours of guidance, support, advice and inspiration. Chisnall was charged with using the premises for 'public dancing', allegedly in breach of his licence, and fined £10. The prosecution described the club as 'dirty, dimly lit with a foul atmosphere and music so loud that even a shouted conversation was impossible'. Letters of support – including one from Leslie Wilkins, former deputy director of a Home Office research unit and by that time Professor of Criminology at California University – were produced in court to highlight Chisnall's valuable efforts in youth work. In a letter to a friend, Arthur wrote of his ongoing struggle to keep up the work he was devoted to:

> After all these years it has suddenly 'been discovered' that we do not come up to licensing regulations. We are trying to find out what is going to be needed before we are allowed to carry on, but already know that it will involve a new floor and a number of other repairs and alterations costing at least £2,000.
>
> I was in the process of forming a trust with the aim of buying and utilising the whole hotel. Unfortunately the present situation means that instead of being able to do this, it is now doubtful as to whether I shall be able to continue at all, which is rather sad as I just seemed to be reaching the point where the island was being recognised as a potential model for our youth services.

Chisnall took his work home with him. His house in nearby Strawberry Hill had already become an extension of the club, an 'open house' providing support and understanding to a continual flow of people. But closure of the club, his only source of income,

'I started going there in the early Sixties. Saw some great bands and had some **wild** times! It was really quite safe there, but, you know, there were some "diverse characters", some of whom you wouldn't have wanted to get to know any better. And some of the girls – well, I thought I was wild until I went there. I had to up my game a few notches! I remember seeing Alexis Korner . . . It was almost like the island was a spaceship and we were all just encapsulated with this **fantastic** music, on this gorgeous summer evening, lying on the grass smoking loads of dope, just thinking, **"This is it!"'** *Jo Matthews*

jeopardised this too.

> My income to support the house, where at the moment we are looking after at least a dozen people, has stopped. We are negotiating with the Ministry of Social Security, trying to get them to take on some of the costs. After all it is their work we are doing, but officialdom moves very slowly.

Arthur applied for a new licence, but the club never opened its welcoming doors again. According to a close friend, he tried on a few occasions to buy the freehold of the hotel, but became increasingly frustrated by Michael Snapper always pricing it 'just beyond his reach'. Aware that planning permission for development would yield far more money than he could ever raise, Chisnall suspected that he was 'just a pawn in the game between Snapper and the council as Snapper sought permission to redevelop'. The local establishment were, by and large, anti-Eelpiland and its bohemian/beatnik/hippie associations; one member of the local police force, in particular, was determined to see its doors slammed shut for good. The club's closure was the beginning of the end for a once-magnificent structure – had it happened today, the building would surely have been protected by listed building status.

Arthur Chisnall continued with his quest to provide solutions that worked for the young and for those

ABOVE: Dave Brock with friends in the hotel grounds, 1960.

RIGHT: Dave Brock wrings out his t-shirt: sometimes it was quicker (and cheaper by 4d) to swim to the island!

'Lying in the summer sunshine on the lawn listening to the band, or being chased by Jack Mars who ran the hotel bar, for doing something illegal' John Platt

'Does anyone remember trying to get lucky outside, when the police would sail past and turn a spotlight on the gardens?' Neil Bryson

who did not fit in to society's structure. He had contacts at the Home Office and at various universities in Britain and abroad who were all drawing upon his experience and methods of working with young people. He became actively involved with the BIT Information Service (named after a 'bit', the smallest unit of information in computing terms). Run by youth for youth, BIT gave information on anything and everything, free. No big deal by today's Google standards – but back then, as Arthur's friend Auriol McKay explained:

> BIT was a very radical concept. Information in those days was not always readily available and so was seen as the new freedom. Despite Arthur probably being the oldest man to step through its doors, he used his charisma to become a front-man for BIT, liaising with established services such as the police. He secured charitable status for BIT and also got them a grant from the Gulbenkian Foundation. Arthur was very enthusiastic about groups like these; he saw them as a new society in the

ABOVE RIGHT: Club members and their guests in the hotel gardens.

OVERLEAF: Painting of the hotel during its days as a hippie commune.

making. A major part of his life's work was to create bridges between people in need and established organisations. He was a networker before his time – his phone rang constantly. He also went on to be instrumental, along with his friend Jack Lambert, in setting up some of the first adventure playgrounds both here and in Berlin.

BAREFOOT COLONELS, THE COMMUNE & THE END OF AN ERA

Early in May 1968 Snapper reopened the Eel Pie Hotel, initially without a licence to serve alcohol. According to a police representative at the licence application hearing, the venue was 'still in a deplorable condition. Paint had been put on top of dirty and rotting woodwork and the general effect was one of covering up instead of putting right the structural defects.'

The rift between Snapper and Chisnall was continuing, with the former telling the *Middlesex Chronicle*: 'Mr Chisnall did quite a lot of good. If he wants to

combine with his contacts on Richmond upon Thames Council and run a youth centre on the island I'll have no objection. In fact I'll offer him every facility.' To which Chisnall replied, 'As far as I'm concerned I'm still banned – no direct approach has been made to me.'

The venue was briefly used by Richmond Arts Workshop to hold a few dances with the specific aim of paying rent for the ballroom and putting on future arts events. Mark Newton, also known as Caldwell Smythe, a larger than life promoter/manager, was apparently happy to give the impression that he owned the whole hotel: he muscled in and rapidly took over. Renaming the venue 'Colonel Barefoot's Rock Garden', he ran it as a purely commercial venture. The new name came from the footprints that adorned the ceiling of the bar.

Although in no way comparable to the original club hosted by Arthur, the new club is remembered affectionately by many folk who had great, often drug-fuelled, times there. Noteworthy bands such as Hawkwind, Deep Purple, Atomic Rooster, The Edgar Broughton Band, Black Sabbath, Rory Gallagher and The Who took to the stage. Colonel Barefoot's shared none of the altruistic motives of Chisnall, and for some of those who had been into R 'n' B and jazz the transition to psychedelia and prog rock was all too much. John Platt lamented in *Comstock Lode*:

It was pretty sleazy in comparison with the old

'**We badly needed a place to live** with our kids Filip and Ama. We heard about Eel Pie from a friend in Kensington Market. There were two guys at the hotel acting as caretakers and they were welcoming to everyone – when we got there that day all the rooms were empty still, except for maybe one . . . It was so beautiful, a venerable, classy old hotel which even had a ballroom with a rock 'n' roll history, a **dreamy setting** on the river, swans, ducks – we couldn't believe it was real. We picked a room and moved in immediately. Within a week all the rooms were occupied, the hotel was full of people – all so different yet all with so many ideas in common. It was fantastic' *Felix and Loretta Leu, who moved in to the hotel in September 1969. The Leu family found fame as tattoo artists, and Filip is now widely respected as one of the world's greatest exponents of this art form*

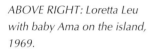

ABOVE RIGHT: Loretta Leu with baby Ama on the island, 1969.

club, a strictly commercial operation featuring those ghastly English rock bands for whom 1969 was the big year – Stray, Black Sabbath, Edgar Broughton, etc. Half the audience were police in long-haired wigs. Also you had to walk back past the Bird's Nest pub where skin-heads used to throw people through plate glass windows for the fun of it.

By the late summer of 1969, the main body of the hotel was occupied by an assortment of alternative-lifestyle seekers. According to one of the commune's founders, Clifford Harper, squatters they were not: they paid Michael Snapper rent. 'Snapper would climb out of his Rolls, cross the bridge and wander around trying to collect fivers. Sometimes he'd be satisfied, sometimes he wouldn't.'

Clifford was a committed anarchist and a veteran of a commune in Cumbria; along with half a dozen others he took up residence in the crumbling hotel.

I was a friend of Arthur Chisnall, who pointed us to Eel Pie and suggested we move in. Various ideas were initially discussed along the lines of setting up an arts lab but they quickly dissolved back into the air, where they'd come from. Things just went their own way.

By the following summer, Eel Pie Island's redis-covered notoriety as a place for free living, free love and free-your-mind drugs had served to attract over a hundred people who made it their home. A core

group was dedicated to communal and anarchist ideals, but there were also plenty of hangers-on and part-timers. Clifford Harper wrote in *The Education of Desire* about middle-class hippies who

would slope off to their parents' suburban homes for a bath and to use the washing machine at the weekend. They were incredibly furtive about it. I thought they were estab-lishing contacts with some other commune somewhere, but in fact they were all off for a bit of R and R.

Even though the hotel offered ample space, the number of people eventually calling it home took communal living to extremes; inevitably, what little order that could exist in such a free and anarchic environment all but disappeared. The inhabitants began to cannibalise the very structure of their home. By the winter of 1970–71, with gas and electricity cut off, the nearest available source of fuel to heat the building was the building itself. Timber was ripped from floors, walls, stairs or anywhere within reach, and burned for warmth. Michael Snapper began to lose any altruistic notions he might have had when he saw the rack and ruin caused by the inhabitants. His son Emile recalled going over there and witnessing the destruction:

I saw them pulling up the floorboards and lighting fires in their rooms with them. I remember thinking, 'Well, that's a little bit

'**My friend Nigel and I** used to set up our psychedelic light show called "Aural Plasma" there in 1969–70. The guy running it then, Mark, was a real mad character who had studied judo in Japan, drove a white Jag and had an Alsatian dog that he would introduce by saying, "Tickle his bollocks, he likes it"! We had some **crazy, drug-induced nights** there with Black Sabbath, Mott the Hoople and many others. Mark made a vicious "Colonel Barefoot's punch"; I never did find out what was in it. We were paid about £20 for two nights' work, but we didn't care, it was just great fun to be around this scene. The hotel part was a squat; I didn't like going in there, it freaked me out. They used to steal electricity from the club, which caused a few **angry scenes**'   *Michael*

'**An acceptably out of control** international crash-pad, with many people arriving there via BIT. The dancehall [Colonel Barefoot's] and the commune maintained an **uneasy alliance**, with commune members given free access to the dances for a while, but eventually the interconnecting doors were locked and the two groups went their separate ways. Many people who came to the dances would also pay a visit to the commune though, to score some dope'   *Weed, commune member*

LEFT: Commune members outside the hotel. Founder-member Clifford Harper recalls that 'Sally McLean, being very fit and athletic, was the first through a small window beside the main door, which she then opened and Simon Dunne and myself walked in. It was about 11 a.m, I think it was a Tuesday, 1969.'

'**Once someone donated** a van-load of food. No one questioned it. We just carried it over the footbridge, like a trail of ants, back to the nest. It was stacked up against the wall along the first-floor corridor. I mainly remember the stacks of trays of eggs and boxes of corn-on-the-cob but there was a variety of foodstuff. At the top of the first flight of stairs was a room we called "the kitchen" even though there were no facilities, just a small calor gas cooker. For three days and nights there was a queue of people wanting to use that cooker, then all the food was gone. The word had got out, and dossers and freaks came from all around the area to partake in the **free food**. The gas bottle had to be changed several times during those three days. Sometimes in the middle of the night someone would go and wake up Mrs Brock because she had a little tea room and sold bottled gas.

'It turned out that the food was a kind of **bribe**. Suddenly the garden was filled with a sea of tents, including a tipi which had been tie-dyed in a swimming pool. It was done in earthy colours, mostly green with flecks of red and yellow, incorporating huge circles and sunbursts. We were very impressed and our number was more than doubled overnight. This was the famous Hog Farm Commune from America – well, half of them at least; the other half landed on a commune in North London. They came to buy two London buses to travel to India in. Nobody remembered that the very high tides could sometimes cover the garden; one morning all their tents got **flooded**'

Dominic McCormack, commune member

silly.' My father got really annoyed at this and he wanted them out. He just couldn't understand why they would want to do it.

Although some readily described Snapper as 'only in it for the money', he told the press that he 'would do all he could for the hippies even though they had long stopped paying any rent'. He said he would give them six months' notice and was happy to let them stay on through the winter, as many of them had nowhere else to go. 'Conditions at the hotel may not be perfect, but at least they've got a roof over their heads,' he said. Weed, a commune member, commented in *Met OJ on Eel Pie '69*:

Maybe he assumed that it would just be a matter of time before the council realised that the only way to get rid of the unwashed hordes that had descended on the place was to have it demolished. I suspect that as well as being a successful local businessman, he was something of a bohemian and still retained more than a streak of libertarian humour.

Around November 1970 the hotel was declared unfit for human habitation, and Social Services was debating whether to serve a demolition order. The NSPCC were called in, but concluded that the children there were all happy, healthy and well cared for.

In January 1971 Snapper was fined £150 for 'allowing public music and dancing to be held in the ballroom without holding a GLC licence'. The same month, the cellar was flooded and he was forced to turn off the water supply. He expressed sad bewilderment at the destructive actions of the commune members and gave them notice to quit. The council decided to serve an official demolition order on the weary building, to be effective within 12 weeks.

Clifford Harper recalled the commune's downfall:
The big destructive force was the speed freaks, who were all lightweight criminals. In the winter of 1970–71, which is when it began to get really harsh and hard, they brought the place down. Most of those that had generated the original collective and communal notions were gone by then and all the middle-class hippies had left for pastures new, so they didn't experience the collapse. Also, the pressure from the good burghers of Twickenham, who did not like us, and the Richmond Drug Squad, getting pretty strident from the summer of 1970 onwards – all [this] added to the eventual demise.

Clifford stayed there up to February 1971, when he was hospitalised for three months with tuberculosis. He went on to become a self-taught artist, illustrating many radical publications. His striking work has appeared in many national newspapers and his 'Country Diary' illustrations for the *Guardian* have made him one of their most popular artists.

There are as many versions of what happened next

ABOVE: A commune dweller crosses the bridge. The Mini-van visible on the island was the only vehicle licensed by the council to cross, in order to deliver coal. The pedestrian bridge was just wide enough for that iconic Sixties motor!

as there are people left to recall them. On 2 March 1971 a planning application was submitted for a housing development on the hotel site. On the morning of 30 March 1971, fire broke out at the hotel. Conspiracy theories abound. 'Obviously an insurance job,' many asserted then and later, but this notion was laughed at by Emile Snapper:

> There was no insurance! In those days if you weren't using it you didn't insure it. . . . It was the hippies who set fire to the place and my father was really hurt; it was something he had bought and a place he loved; he was hurt that someone should destroy it.

But Clifford Harper is in no doubt that Snapper was behind the fire:

> He did nothing to prevent the extensive damage done. That's what we were supposed to do. He initially thought that 'hippies' in the heart of bourgeois Twickenham would push the council into accepting his plans for redevelopment. When this didn't happen he was forced to the ancient developer's tactic of arson. I did hear that he'd paid some of the speed freaks to set the fire.

Chisnall recalled:

> When the community living there got out of hand he encouraged it by the mere fact that he didn't do anything about it. There's this myth about a massive fire, but it was just a small,

controlled blaze used to accelerate the demolition process, and a bit of a PR exercise really.

Newspapers reported that the hotel was empty of dwellers, with the demolition team already hard at work when the flames took hold. A police spokesman told the *Richmond and Twickenham Times:* 'The fire was caused when a bonfire, lit by demolition workers to burn rubbish, got out of hand.'

THE END OF AN ERA

Michael Snapper continued with his go-getting lifestyle. He was still taking part in the London to Brighton car rally well into his 90s, went abseiling at 91 and was planning on water skiing to celebrate his 100th birthday, but he died on 13 December 2006, aged 98. Barely two weeks later, on 28 December, Arthur Chisnall also died, aged 81, after a short spell in the Princess Alice Hospice in Esher. He was given a splendid send-off to the swinging sounds of New Orleans jazz.

The musical spirit of Eelpiland was revived when the Eel Pie Club was formed in 2000. Playing host at the nearby Cabbage Patch pub to numerous musicians and old 'islanders' who had spent many happy nights there in the Sixties, as well as a younger crowd of new converts, the club is fulfilling its aim of preserving and continuing the heritage of British Rhythm and Blues in the area where it all began.

'**I feel very sad** to have seen the old hotel burning away like this. It has always been a wonderful place as far as I was concerned'
Michael Snapper

'**Michael obviously**, and rightly, saw the potential fortune to be made from redevelopment'
Arthur Chisnall

Part 3
The Age of Aquarius

Dan van der Vat

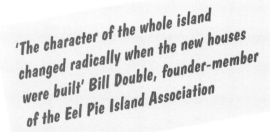

'The character of the whole island changed radically when the new houses were built' Bill Double, founder-member of the Eel Pie Island Association

ALL CHANGE

The demise of the hotel on Eel Pie Island and its replacement by an estate of town houses implies a simple transition from bohemia to suburbia. And so, in an obvious sense, it was; but not altogether. For example, Brock's Tea Garden, built in 1928, stayed in business (of a sort) in spectacularly crumbling premises until its owner, Mrs Ada Argent, died in 1983. The place was frequently flooded until an island campaign successfully persuaded the Greater London Council in 1980 to build individual flood defences for the nine island properties most at risk. The property, Min-y-Don, was bought by the architect Clive Chapman, who has constructed a handsome family house and a separate modern studio there.

Bill Double and his late mother, Cecilia, moved into Hurley Cottage, a pretty clapboard house, in 1966. He remembers how

> the hotel was a place to avoid in those days. It still had a bar and there were a few people living in the rooms, but it was falling apart and overgrown. It became a hippie squat . . .

The Doubles helped to found the Eel Pie Island Association (EPIA) at the beginning of the 1970s. Its original purpose was to collect islanders' contributions to the communal water bill, because Thames Water delivered to the island as a whole and did not levy individual water rates. Until separate water meters were installed in the older premises in the mid-1980s, there were many disputes, sometimes about tiny amounts of money, and about what 'fair shares' meant, especially when the communal bill rose with inflation: one late resident refused ever to increase his payment from what he paid when the scheme started. Shortly before the meters arrived there was an extraordinary row at an EPIA annual general meeting, which became known as the 'battle of the pacemakers'. Three frail, elderly gentlemen argued the toss about who should pay what with such intensity that the rest of those attending feared for their health. A shocked committee resigned en bloc.

By the time I was elected chairman in 2000 (until 2005), meetings were rather more decorous and there were no more arguments about the water supply. A separate water pipe serves the Aquarius development and adjacent working premises, but so far no individual meters have been installed there. Aquarius Riverside Ltd, which owns the freehold of the estate and is run by the residents, pays a communal bill. The anarchic spirit of the island may not be anything like as apparent as it was before the 1971 fire, but it is still to be found among a shifting population of houseboat dwellers and the artists and craftspeople who remained to live or work on the island after the hotel was demolished, not least in the boatyards. Even the musical tradition was briefly recalled, albeit in a different form, with the Mystery Jets pop band.

'People like you shouldn't buy motor boats. You'd be much better off standing on the river bank and chucking in £20 notes. That's much less stressful – and a lot cheaper' Sound advice from Bill Sims

The fire at the hotel marked its complete demise after 141 years, and left only a shell. Michael Snapper had made a planning application exactly four weeks before the blaze and had been thinking of building houses well before then: one early vision was for a larger, vehicular bridge, 66 homes, 77 garages and a restaurant with six flats above, all to house 380 people on 5½ acres.

The outcome, after many vicissitudes – including the bankruptcy of Edinburgh House Developments who started work on the plan – was a small estate of two-storey houses with river frontage, in three staggered blocks of six. The council would not allow three storeys or a road bridge; residents had to leave their cars on the Embankment. The houses were put on the market in the mid 1970s by Snapper, who had taken over the building work from a company called Penates Ltd. A large dip in the housing market reduced the asking price from £45,000 to £29,500, which is what I paid for a middle house in the middle block in 1976. In keeping with the spirit of the 1970s, the estate was christened Aquarius. There is a hard in front of the third block, which is set back far enough from the river's edge to allow for the shared Aquarius lawn, used for island picnics; the hard has a numbered slot for each house – 'for a day-boat', as the brochure put it.

BOATS & YARDS

Boats have been a principal feature of life on the island, pre-dating the hotel and continuing long after its disappearance. Boats are still worked on there, if not built. The Thames in London has hardly any working river-front left but, much against the odds, the tradition survives on the island, where the largest facility, Eel Pie Island Slipways Ltd, is still busy. The construction of the half-lock and weir at Richmond in 1894 had ensured that the river was navigable round the clock by boats with shallow draught, regardless of the state of the tide in the river as a whole. This gave more flexibility to pleasure boats, and by extension to the yards that looked after them. It also made life easier for the Twickenham Rowing Club, and for the George Sims Racing Boats company on the island which served rowers for many years, pioneering the use of fibreglass (it has now relocated to Goring-by-Sea, West Sussex; during the war it built marine-ply-hulled motor gunboats). Sims was run for many years by one of the great characters on the island, the late Bill Sims, who in his old age used to walk up and down the main path looking for people to chat to. He consistently denied that he could read or write, yet for years he got a nervous BBC to raise its annual offer (unanswered for weeks) for the hire of the motorboats used by the officials who ran the Oxford and Cambridge Boat Race downriver.

Mrs Mayo's kitchen garden became the site on which William Samuel Sargent of Chiswick, west London, built the sheds and charging station (for electric boats) of the Thames Electric and Steam Launch Company. Shortly after building the largest-ever electric boat, the *Victory*, the company was forced to call in a receiver, in 1906. Joseph Mears bought the business in 1907, operating launches as well as building and maintaining them. When Mears died suddenly in 1935 his company owned 28 boats. He was also a local councillor and chairman of Chelsea Football Club (as was his more famous son, Joe). Several Mears boats joined the 'little ships' that took part in the miraculous evacuation of the British army from Dunkirk in June 1940. Naval landing craft were built in his yard.

Just before the end of the war, Joseph Mears Launches and Motors Ltd was sold to Thames Launches Ltd. In 1956 the company spawned Thames Launch Works Ltd (Impala Marine Ltd from 1973), hiving off building from the operating element. In 1966 the Port of London Authority (PLA), which controls the Thames tideway, decided to increase its fees by 40 per cent, with further increases of 10 per cent for each of the next five years, thus laying the foundations of an unfortunate reputation for rapacity which is very much alive at the time of writing.

At the end of the 1960s, Thames Launch Works started an enterprising search for work abroad, winning orders for various specialised shallow-water or river craft from far-flung countries. It also built large tugs and enough pleasure steamers to retain a leading place in that industry. At the end of 1977, Thames Launch Works and Impala Marine decided to withdraw from the pleasure-boat business and the fleet was sold off. The firm allegedly owed the government some £350,000 in export credits when Impala closed in July 1979 (it was finally struck off the company register in 1983).

The successor company was Strong Marine Construction, set up by the felicitously named Denis Salmon and John Pike (finance director). Salmon paid the liquidator £4,650 and promised to repay the government. As early as 1981 the company was in trouble, unable to balance its books; some workers agreed not to draw their wages to help, but it was too

late even for such unusual sacrifices. The Export Credit Guarantee Department pressed for the return of its money and finally called in the receivers, who closed the yard and put it up for sale. Even the national press took an interest. The irrepressible Salmon and Pike had formed a company called Tourist Leisure and through it bid £140,000 for the business, £5,000 more than an offer made by a group of employees, who were not pleased when the identity of their rival's directors was revealed.

The employees prevailed: Len Bowman and Ted Leppard took over the core of the site as Eel Pie Island Slipways Ltd in 1984. The western end was sold for the construction of the largest house on the island, Palm Beach, and the eastern end went to the Australian-born entrepreneur Henry Gastall, a man somewhat in the Michael Snapper mould, who had cut his teeth in the antiques business. He turned out to be in the Arthur Chisnall mould also: he employed disabled and disadvantaged people and encouraged them to improve their environment and their own prospects, also allowing other denizens of the workshops and studios to borrow space and tools for their various enterprises. He set up the Eel Pie Marine Centre in 1983, offering facilities for private boatowners to repair and generally tinker with their craft. There were also pontoons, berths for houseboats, a primitive toilet block and a warren of studios and workshops in a raggle-taggle of buildings immedi-

ately to the east of the large shed and slipway owned by Eel Pie Island Slipways. This amiably shambolic organism with its motley gallery of unconventional occupants endured until the great fire of 1996.

Among them was my co-author, Michele Whitby, invited by friends to visit the centre in 1988 after studying photography for three years. She fell for the place and took over a studio. Michele eventually turned from photography to making upmarket leather goods – until the fire of 1996 destroyed her stock.

Thereafter Gastall sold about half the site to a developer called Henry Harrison who, with the fire in mind, renamed his easterly portion Phoenix Wharf. Some years later Harrison also bought the Sims boatbuilding site, Sans Souci, for redevelopment. Underestimating the complexity and sensitivity of the overlapping interests on the island, he managed to antagonise many of his neighbours, at least until he adopted a rather more sensitive public relations policy. Meanwhile, he helped his physically handicapped son to set up the Mystery Jets band, himself playing with them when they began rehearsing noisily at Phoenix Wharf. The band achieved nationwide publicity and plenty of gigs.

The other part of the former Marine Centre went to the Montgomery-Smith family, who had worked there and who now set up the Eel Pie Boatyard at the western end, offering a dry dock and a crane, a workshop, pontoons and moorings for houseboats. The EP

OPPOSITE: Boatyards such as Eel Pie Island Slipways have long been a key part of island life; they have faced constant pressure from developers.

LION BOATHOUSE
TEL. 0181- 891. 1025
MOORINGS, SLIPWAY & D.I.Y.

LEFT: Boatyard during a bad patch in the 1970s. The Lion Boathouse was long owned by the late Sandy Scott, an island resident for over fifty years.

RIGHT: Ivy Castle, a
beautiful south-facing
Victorian wooden house,
has its own dock entrance
for houseboats.

Boatyard is the last main refuge of the cheerful chaos that once had most of the island in its grip: strange wreckage litters the ground, including the entire upper works of a small motor-vessel, complete with red funnel. To reach Phoenix Wharf you have to cross land owned by EPI Slipways; to reach the EP Boatyard, you have to pass the territory of both. Hazards such as general clutter and steel cables have to be negotiated. A certain tolerance is needed by and for all concerned, as Harrison discovered.

Meanwhile, EPI Slipways was sold by Bowman and Leppard to Thames Cruises Ltd, which keeps it as a facility for repairing and maintaining its own riverboats, along with those owned by some half-dozen other operators. The yard is operated by Ken Dwan, a prominent figure among the Thames Watermen, and his wife Kate, who set up a boat service for local Hindus and Sikhs, enabling them to deposit the ashes of their relatives in the Thames – which was declared a tributary of the Ganges for the purpose!

Before they took over, EPI Slipways was the setting for a poignant tragedy in February 1993. Bowman's son Keith was working on the hull of a boat when a supporting girder broke through the old concrete floor and the boat heeled over slightly. Keith was trapped between the hull and the wall. The emergency services fought to release him, an air ambulance landed on the Aquarius hard, and all concerned struggled for more than an hour to save him, but to no avail.

Of the other island yards, the Lion Boathouse was owned for decades by Sandy Scott, a great island character since his arrival in 1952, who died soon after he sold out to an architect in 2005; it no longer functions as a boatyard. The handsome Victorian wooden house called Ivy Castle has a small dock which is reached by a channel that runs under the house and fills up at high tide. There is space (just) for eight houseboats and a workshop. This yard was owned and operated by Sebastian Bell, a renowned flautist and professor of music, and his wife Lis, until his premature death in 2007. Lastly, there is the Cruisemaster yard, owned and leased out by the borough of Richmond since the days when a bridge over the mainstream to Ham, Surrey, was under consideration before and after the Second World War. One or two of the handful of small businesses that used to operate in the yard still remain, including the rainbow-coloured wooden hut of the extraordinary commercial caterer and cook known to all as Alafiah, originally from Gambia.

On Sunday 3rd November a horrific fire destroyed the livelihoods of some sixty artists and crafts people working on Eel Pie Island, Twickenham. They formed a unique community of creative and entrepreneurial talent, with a growing reputation for high quality work.

The community comprised a broad range of artistic and practical skills, from artists to violin makers, boat builders to sculptors.

Many of these people lost, not just their place of work, but their tools, portfolios, records and finished pieces.

They also lost an environment where skills were pooled or exchanged, which created a co-operative community of unusual dynamism. Most difficult to reconcile and communicate is the enormous sense of loss felt by everyone who had experienced the special alchemy of the place. Eel Pie Island had soul.

Within twelve hours of the disaster, an appeal was launched for the immediate relief of those involved. Workspace, tools, materials, work and money were requested. Volunteers organised the free production of posters and their free publication in the national press. An appeals and press office was operational within one day.

The appeal has received television, radio and print press coverage both locally and nationally.

The response to the appeal has been fantastic and already workspace has been found for many of the artists.

Within one week of the fire, a Board of Trustees was formed to give the new organisation full legal status and accountability.

The purpose of the appeal is twofold: first, to enable those individuals who have lost their livelihood to return to work, second to keep the spirit of Eel Pie Island alive.

The Trustees wish to investigate ways of rebuilding what was lost on the island.

Obviously the immediate concern of everyone involved has been to put people back on their feet. It has been estimated the appeal needs around £9,000 to get the community back to work.

Everyone is aware that we need to raise larger sums of money now or the dream will die, the community will dissipate and Eel Pie Island could become just another housing redevelopment.

LEFT: Pages from the brochure produced by the Eel Pie Trust after the fire of 1996. Generous donations of financial and practical aid came from many sources and memorable events were organised to help the sixty or so people whose livelihoods had been destroyed.

THE GREAT FIRE

In the early hours of Sunday 3 November 1996, my elder daughter and her visiting German girlfriend were awakened, not by noise but by heat. They were in the two bedrooms at the front of our house in Aquarius, the closest on the estate to the south wall of the EPI Slipways shed. Only a few yards from their beds a fierce fire was raging. They woke my wife and me, blithely asleep at the back of the house, and we all looked out of the upstairs front windows in horror. Firemen were dousing the east wall of the yard to prevent the high flames from the Marine Centre from engulfing it. This saved the yard and the boats inside it even as the adjacent premises were destroyed. Some gallant residents and craftspeople rushed in to remove gas canisters – calor, propane, oxy-acetylene – which might otherwise have gone off like bombs, blasting shrapnel in all directions. At 3 a.m. the police ordered an evacuation and we all trooped over the footbridge. St Mary's church hall was opened up for us, and island resident Bruce Lyons kindly threw open his business premises at Crusader Travel in nearby Church Street. Much tea was drunk as a grand total of 37 fire appliances came and went, including a great fire-boat that eventually sailed up from the Pool of London. When we were allowed to return to the island at breakfast-time, we had no idea of what we were going to find.

The Marine Centre was almost entirely destroyed; but the main boatyard and Aquarius had been saved by a strong southerly wind, driving the flames northward and away from us, and by the defensive efforts of the fire crews. For the same reasons, a row of studios on the southern perimeter of the site and the toilet block survived unscathed.

Michele Whitby had been running her leather-goods workshop on the island for several years:

ABOVE: The morning after: the 'Ashtray' site on 4 November 1996. Many fought to recover what had been lost, but after countless hours attending council planning meetings and writing letters of objection, Trust members, residents of the island and others lost their cause. The burnt-out part of the site was eventually developed into a gated, sterile, luxury office complex, with all evidence of light industrial and boatyard use gone forever.

In the early hours of Sunday 3 November a huge fire swept through Eel Pie Marine Centre. The timber buildings were quickly engulfed by the soaring flames that embraced the many gas bottles used for welding and heating, causing an explosive atmosphere that was incredibly dangerous for the fire crews to enter. By dawn all that was left was a smouldering heap of burnt-out livelihoods.

My baby son, Louie, was six weeks old at the time, so I was at home . . . I was woken at 4 a.m. by friends who told me: 'Come quickly, the boatyard's on fire!' I went and stood in disbelief on the Embankment and watched as the place went up. I had my biggest-ever order, for 300 suede baseball caps, half-finished in my workshop. The next day all that remained were the metal stairs that had led to my door.

Most people had been partying at one of Trevor Baylis's legendary bashes so at least nobody was injured, or worse, in the fire, but the reality that greeted us all the next day was shocking and sobering.

Arson was strongly suspected, but despite the arrest of a suspect nothing was proved. The sixty artists and craftspeople who lost their livelihoods that terrible night were almost all uninsured: no insurer would contemplate providing cover for premises that were the ultimate nightmare for the health and safety fraternity. Thousands of pounds invested in equipment, materials and products went up in smoke.

The victims of the blaze reacted with commendable determination, speed and efficiency. I was approached the evening after the catastrophe by three of the people affected to help launch an appeal. As a journalist I was asked to write a media handout

Furniture Maker Robert Bannon · **Painter** Bea · **Painter** Carolyn Bew · **Instrument Maker** Simon Birkett · **Potter** James Burnett-Stuart · **Packaging Designers/Cartoonists** Guy Campbell and Paul Moran · **Costume Designer** Rosa Dias · **Antique Furniture Restorers** Nick Dyson and Mark Baker · **Painter/Printmaker** Melanie Epps · **Sculptor** Guy Hardern · **Cartographer** Cathy Horton · **Sculptor** Michael Jensen · **Jeweller** Margaret Kane · **Painter** Sue Knight · **Jeweller** Astrid Mahrer · **Sculptor** Emily Morgan · **Painter** Margaret Morrison · **Photographer** Ralph **Photographer** Clive Rowat · **Potter** Judith Rowe · **Blacksmith** Nick Shields · **Painter** James Tuttle · **Furniture Designers & Bronzecasters** Paul Verburg and Barbara Brownfield · **Leatherworker** Michelle Whitby · **Painter** Anna Williams.

INVITE YOU TO

THE EEL PIE CHRISTMAS SHOW

Saturday 9th December   Sunday 10th December, 11 - 7 pm

Eel Pie Marine Centre, Eel Pie Island, Twickenham, Middlesex TW1 3DY
Telephone: 0181 892 3626

These are working studios in a busy boatyard. Any accompanying children must be closely supervised.

Please bring this invitation with you

which was quickly distributed that very night. The appeal office was set up at the back of the Par-Ici shop in Church Street, Twickenham (this had begun as an outlet for goods produced on or near Eel Pie Island, and is now managed by Michele Whitby). Within a week, a board of trustees was formed and support was pouring in, not only from local people but also from much further afield, including many show-business stars, who remembered and in some cases participated in the island's musical past. The appeal soon raised more than £40,000, which was distributed to victims who needed help to re-start their enterprises.

For months the site of the fire, nicknamed the Ashtray, was covered in blackened detritus. A scorched chimney column made of brick stood alone, the wooden building it had served completely consumed by the flames. A few came back; a good score of artists and craftspeople now have premises on the EP Boatyard site. They hold regular public showings of their work, as used to occur before the blaze. But it is a much more subdued affair than before, a shadow of past richness.

As part of a valiant effort to control the blaze, which took several hours, firefighters from the London Fire Brigade had come from all over the city. Four strong men, one at each corner, had carried a heavy pump over the footbridge by hand, because the seat of the fire was more than 300 yards from Twick-enham Embankment, the nearest point to park their engines. With this pump they could make use of river water, as well as the water brought over the bridge and along the main path by hoses from their appliances. In bringing the pump over, the firefighters ignored the restriction on the bridge of no more than three pedestrians at a time, which had been imposed by Richmond Council because the structure was gravely weakened.

This brings us to the other great island crisis of the 1990s: the mortal threat to the bridge, without which the entire community – residents, businesses and the two boating clubs – would wither away.

THE FOOTBRIDGE: DEATH & REBIRTH

The Snapper Bridge had transformed not only the fortunes of the Eel Pie Island Hotel but also the character of the island itself. Now the cottages were readily accessible and, with Twickenham railway station just a ten-minute walk away (a twenty-odd minute ride to Waterloo), they became attractive to commuters, especially when Aquarius was built. But when damage done to the bridge by the attachment of a gas pipe in 1987 was discovered in 1993, the island's link to the rest of the world, taken for granted for 36 years, was suddenly under serious threat. Ever resourceful, the EPIA set up a Bridge Action Committee (BAC). My own role on it was public and media relations.

The cachet of most distinguished island resident – notwithstanding Trevor Baylis, William Hartnell (the first Dr Who in the 1960s) and Nigel Planer (Neil in *The Young Ones* in the 1990s) – must go to the late **Sir Jocelyn Bodilly** (left), once Chief Justice of the Western Pacific, who moved into Aquarius in 1975. He and his wife set off each summer in their finery to Buckingham Palace for the Queen's garden party, but they were no 'stuffed shirts'. My wife and I were invited round to advise Sir Jocelyn on a Latin motto for his coat of arms. An unexpectedly well-lubricated and hilarious evening ensued as we mulled over a series of Latin tags with more and more outrageous **double meanings**. Lady Bodilly displayed a robust sense of humour when a young man swam to the island for a bet – and proved his success by 'borrowing' **her underwear** from the washing-line. As a student in Germany in 1933, Bodilly and a teacher smuggled the radical German-Jewish educationist Kurt Hahn to Switzerland in the back of a car; Hahn went on to found Gordonstoun school. Bodilly served in the RNVR during the Second World War and then joined the colonial legal service. The couple retired to Cornwall in 1985; she died in 1996 and a devastated Sir Jocelyn just one year later.

ABOVE: Sir Jocelyn Bodilly in loquacious mode.

OVERLEAF: Some of the highly individual island houses built before the Aquarius era, showing the unusual architectural tastes of Eel Pie's residents. Top, left to right: Wyndfall, Run Softly, Tideway, Love Shack (formerly Rose Cottage), Desdemona. Bottom, left to right: The Nook, Woodford, The Sycamores, Min-y-Don.

The good news was that the island boasted an array of professionals who willingly joined the exhausting campaign: a former senior BP executive, Jack Betteridge, took the chair in turn with the late John Gladstone, an architect and planning expert and absolute master of detail; they saw the campaign through to its hard-won victory. As well as a jobbing journalist, they recruited a civil engineer, two more architects, a lawyer and several others – including the man who eventually supplied our secret weapon, the insurance loss adjuster Edward Davies.

The bad news was that it took us five years and four months to win the argument, involving endless meetings among ourselves and with various representatives of British Gas, Richmond Council (who proved to be sympathetic and usually helpful), a barrister and Giffords, the builders of the bridge, to name but four. The first problem was that the island population, whose homes or livelihoods depended on the bridge, were legally bystanders; Michael Snapper, however, the owner whose property had been damaged by an agent of British Gas, took no interest in the rescue effort. Snapper graciously allowed the islanders to spend their money on his bridge, even though his claim to own it was, at the least, debatable. The bridge seemed to be an orphan: if there was no legal owner, it could fall into the hands of the Treasury Solicitor, but that official washed his hands of the problem at once, renouncing any interest. Eventually,

a dozen volunteers from among the residents, businesses and clubs put together a few thousand pounds on behalf of the island and bought out Snapper's residual interests.

In February 1994 we received a letter stating: 'British Gas will meet all remedial costs.' Our joy was unconfined – but the euphoria, not for the last time in this saga, was premature. Everyone took their time, but things seemed set to go ahead in March 1995. Three months later, British Gas made a cash offer of £81,085.32 to the BAC. Giffords having advised us that such an unusual contract could overrun by as much as 40 per cent, we refused. Ownership of the bridge and the main path was eventually transferred in November 1995 to an off-the-peg company rejoicing in the entirely inappropriate name of Tower of Power Ltd (ToP), supported by residents, businesses and the two boating clubs. Letters wound their way to and fro between ToP and Transco, the newly relevant offshoot of British Gas, while the bridge continued to deteriorate. Eventually, Giffords said that the concrete span would have to be removed altogether and a steel structure substituted.

Richmond Council was now proposing to close the bridge for safety reasons. As early as February 1994 they had ordered their refuse collectors not to cross it, and residents had the choice of taking rubbish off the island themselves or letting it accumulate in stinking heaps. As public relations officer I had

no difficulty in gaining massive coverage of our plight, and the council finally laid on a boat to collect rubbish from the Aquarius hard once a week. The adverse publicity about the state of the bridge prompted Transco to stump up £2,000 for a security gate at the Embankment end. From spring 1996, no more than three people or equivalent weight were to be let on to the bridge at any one time.

At this fraught juncture, in May 1996, enter English Heritage, which blithely announced that it planned to give the bridge a Grade II listing because of its unusual design. This could have made a repair prohibitively expensive as it would have to have been identical to the original. The next meddler was the Thames Landscape Strategy, which airily proposed running a path over the bridge, across the island, all the way to the council-owned Cruisemaster yard, where a second bridge would be built over to Ham on the Surrey bank – an old idea, reports of whose death had unfortunately been exaggerated. There was talk of declaring the stretch of the Thames including Richmond and Twickenham a World Heritage site; this would have brought the United Nations, in the

shape of its UNESCO agency, into the staggering complex of interests threatening to engulf our humble little bridge. The joke on the island at the time was to ask why the Vatican, Nato and the European Union were not also involved.

A small but important victory came when we persuaded English Heritage to abandon its listing plan – the first time that it had ever dropped such a proposal, once announced. The Thames Landscape Strategy lost interest when it was made clear that a bridge over the mainstream to Ham would, to permit navigation by the larger pleasure boats, have to be so high above high tide (itself commonly 15 feet or more above low tide) that a tall flight of steps would have to be fitted at either end, to the chagrin of Health and Safety. The Strategy (along with the Millennium people) pleaded lack of funds and withdrew.

Tower of Power applied for permission for a temporary bridge while the permanent one was repaired, and were successful. This was paid for by Transco, while a permanent replacement in steel of the entire structure above the two original piers was planned for the long term. In August 1997, Transco's

ABOVE: The new bridge arrived in two parts on two trucks, was assembled and hoisted by crane at Richmond on to a broad barge, and then towed upstream to the island. With careful attention to the state of the tide, it was delicately manoeuvred into place on the piers, and the wreckage of the old bridge cleared.

ABOVE: Despite having to pay perhaps ten times more than their original cash offer, British Gas/Transco had the grace to lay on a good party at the Rowing Club on the sunny day the new bridge was opened – 8 August 1998. The MP, a vicar and many others were in attendance, including a frail but lively Michael Snapper.

loss adjusters showed they had learned nothing and forgotten nothing: they made a new cash offer of £225,000, well below the lowest tender we had received. We refused. At this tense juncture, Giffords formally advised us that the bridge was unsafe and that we should ask the council to close it. Here was another public relations disaster for Transco, which we exploited to the full. The local and national media took up with enthusiasm the idea of the island that was about to be cut off from Twickenham, London and the world. Our supportive MP, Vincent Cable, came to the well-publicised closure 'ceremony', helping to apply a chain and heavy padlock to the security gate.

Ever resourceful, the island came to its own rescue. Within hours, Ted Leppard of EPI Slipways set up a motorised metal punt as a ferry, available to islanders 24/7; late homecomers had only to call him or his colleague on duty from the Embankment by mobile phone. It ran for 65 days. The bill, to Transco, was £1,000 per day in wages, overtime, fuel, spare parts and a jetty. Then a temporary bridge went up from outside the Barmy Arms to the island, at an angle of 45 degrees to the old bridge.

The campaign reached its peak that August, four days after the ferry service began. At this crucial moment, our own resident loss adjuster, Edward Davies, struck. He produced a priceless precedent, set by the late Lord Denning in the 1970 case of Harbutt's Plasticine v Wayne Tank and Pump. The late Master of the Rolls had ruled that if a second-hand car was damaged one could simply replace it with another second-hand car, whereas if a mill such as the one involved in the case was destroyed (and, by extension, another structure such as a bridge), it could only be rebuilt, and the owners were entitled to full compensation.

Within a week, Transco's loss adjusters returned with an offer to take over the administration of the entire replacement contract, and even to indemnify Tower of Power against any claim arising from the repair. It was a truly sweet victory, all the more so for having been won without recourse to the courts. The new bridge was ceremonially opened on 8 August 1998 and celebrated by one of the great island parties.

EEL PIE ISLAND TODAY

There have been few alarums and excursions since the 'double whammy' of the bridge and the fire in the last years of the old century, although the debate continues about what is to happen to the site facing the north side of the island across the backwater, the former Twickenham open-air swimming pool, closed in 1981. Islanders are heavily involved in the struggle to obtain a sensible solution, so much so that one embattled council official was overheard to say, 'No doubt there'll be another protest from those bastards on Eel Pie Island.' We seem able to punch above our weight, perhaps thanks to the imperishable fame of the musical era. British Gas, the Treasury Solicitor, the council, English Heritage? Let them all come!

Otherwise, every now and again a reporter or a TV crew come to the island for a feature, or to interview Trevor Baylis about his latest invention. The results are frequently as inaccurate as the garbled commentary on the passing pleasure boats. But the fame of the place seems imperishable.

There is a kind of sub-Dunkirk spirit on Eel Pie Island, a strong neighbourly atmosphere which can mean you need half an hour to get to the mainland because of all the people who stop you on the path for a chat. I trace this partly to the fact that the footbridge goes into a dip on the Embankment which is covered by water at unusually high tides. Pedestrians are left with the choice of going to the Barmy Arms for a sociable drink while waiting for the water to go down, or getting their feet wet, or remembering to have wellies handy, or even pulling leaky black binbags over their legs. Strong men gallantly carry ladies over the water, especially if they are pretty and not too heavy. The chance to moan about the tides or about the pressure on local parking space (another inexhaustible topic) is more than enough to encourage the kind of human contact that is demonstrably missing in so many suburbs. When the two topics – high tides and parking – come together and the unwary find their cars full of water, the chat can become very lively indeed. It has happened to all of us . . .

Islanders use an array of trolleys, large and small, to carry over their shopping or the staggering quantities of materials required for the boatyards, the businesses and the many DIY activities on the island, or the formidable supplies of beer and wine to the two boating clubs. Somehow, three baby-grand pianos have been delivered to residents . . .

Three powerful bonding events, not untypical of the island community but highly untypical of almost any other suburb, took place within three weeks in late autumn 2008. A resident couple, Ian and Desna Tyson, celebrated their golden wedding by generously inviting the entire island to their party in the

ABOVE: Trevor Baylis, world-famous inventor of the clockwork radio, and his workshop. Trevor cycled to the island from Southall as a teenager in the 1950s for the jazz. He remembers a tiny old lady in a booth, taking the money as visitors stepped off the chain ferry and stamping their wrists in lieu of tickets. In 1970 he bought a small plot of land at the western end of the island and built a house at the same time as the Aquarius estate was going up. At the back of The Haven is his workshop, while the living room and its picture window face the river. Trevor's once-frequent all-night, all-comers parties kept the old island spirit alive. His 1989 prototype clockwork radio was inspired by the needs of the poor in Africa: unable to afford batteries, they were missing government warnings about Aids.

ABOVE RIGHT: The creative spirit still thrives on Eel Pie Island.

Richmond Yacht Club hall. The turnout was enormous, as it was for the reception after the funeral of Lis Betteridge, wife of Jack. Between these two classic island events, one joyful, one sad but uplifting, was a very enjoyable evening of beer and skittles organised by the Yacht Club at the same venue. Many islanders have hired the hall to celebrate landmark birthdays, and my younger daughter was neither the first nor the last to have her wedding reception there.

Every now and again someone is taken ill and the paramedics have to bring a gurney to convey the patient along the path to the ambulance on the Embankment. The news spreads fast across the island; there cannot be many places where so many neighbours line up to visit you in hospital! I speak from experience . . .

Some say that the Eel Pie world is divided into two categories: those who dislike the island because they cannot park their cars outside the door; and those who love the island, for exactly the same reason. If one must live in a London suburb, one could do a lot worse than choose a little enclave on a traffic-free island in the Thames with an unimpeded view of the open ground of Ham Fields opposite, and just five minutes from the shops, and ten to the railway station. The neighbours are good, too. Probably the only shared regret among the 120 residents and two dozen houseboat dwellers is that the enclave is not larger. Once settled, residents tend to stay . . .

Thanks etc.

We have had a lot of help in the preparation of this book, which could have been three times the length had we been able to use all the material – pictorial, historical and anecdotal – that we were given or offered. We had no choice but to leave out rather more than we included. We are above all grateful to Eel Pie islanders past and present, resident or working, and we apologise in advance to anyone we have omitted below.

Dan van der Vat writes: I owe a special debt of gratitude to (in no particular order) Bill Double, Ian and Desna Tyson, Colin Heath, Ken and Kate Dwan, Georgina Pickard, Bob Hall, James Grantham, Phil and Pam Chart, David Wood, Cathy Horton, the staffs of the local history section of Richmond upon Thames libraries, the London Metropolitan Archives and the National Archives, the *Guardian*, Richmond upon Thames Council.

We are both thankful for the support we have received from our agents at Curtis Brown Ltd (first Jonathan Pegg, then Shaheeda Sabir) and our publishers, Frances Lincoln Ltd, especially Andrew Dunn and Jane Havell.

Michele Whitby writes: First and foremost I want to thank Arthur Chisnall for being an inspiring and obliging friend, and for being such a great hoarder – all the answers to my questions were to be found among the multitude of folders and boxes he kept, and I spent many happy, intriguing hours going through them. I only wish he was still here to see this book finally in print.

So many people have lent their time and support to this project over the years and I sincerely thank everyone who has contributed, helped and encouraged in any way. Particular gratitude must go to Sue Fischer, Weed, Mike Peters, Bill Greenow, Jack Lambert, Derek Griffiths, Tony Leppard, Trevor Baylis, Dave Evans, 'Fluff', Karen O'Brien, Emile Snapper, Dave Palmer, Chris Faiers and, last but not least, Matt, Louie and Leila for putting up with all the piles of paper that have cluttered our living room for the past couple of years.

OPPOSITE: A motto entirely appropriate for the heyday of Eel Pie Island – and not unwelcome today!

These websites may be of interest to the reader:
www.cclpic.org: nostalgia site for all things Eel Pie and a great place to look up old acquaintances
www.kencolyertrust.org: site dedicated to the promotion of New Orleans jazz and Ken Colyer
www.eelpieclub.com: site for the current Richmond Rhythm 'n' Blues club
www.parici.co.uk: Twickenham shop specialising in local arts and crafts, including work from Eel Pie Island artists
www.epia.org.uk: new site set up by the Eel Pie Island Association

Quotations:
p. 42: Ken Colyer, from sleeve notes from a live recording made on the island, May 1957
p. 43: George Melly, from an interview on BBC Radio 4, 2006
p. 64: Todd Allen, from the Cyril Davies tribute website
p. 65: Ian McLagan, from an interview by Jo Meek for *The Eel Pie Island Hotel*, BBC Radio 4, January 2007
p. 82: Chris Faiers, from *Eel Pie Dharma: a memoir/haibun*, Unfinished Monument Press, Toronto, 1990

Pictures:
We are grateful to the following for permission to reproduce pictures (references are to page numbers):

© 2009 Catherine Horton, map on endpapers; courtesy Brian Auger 67 (top left); courtesy Mick Avory 50; courtesy Acker Bilk 42 (bottom); courtesy Dave Brock 51 (both insets), 55, 78 (both); Arthur Chisnall Bequest 30–31, 33, 35, 38–39, 44–45 (all), 53, 56, 59, 62, 67 (contracts), 70 (both insets), 73 (bottom inset), 74, 76, 79, 82; Sian Davies 8–9, 10, 28, 106; T. DiMenno 65; courtesy Bill Double 88, 96 (bottom); courtesy Ken Dwan 19; EPI Fire Appeal Trust 100; courtesy Eel Pie Island Slipways Ltd 96 (top); Chris Faiers 84–85, 87; illustration and calligraphy by Lynne Fisher 24 (both); courtesy 'Fluff' 41; courtesy Derek Griffiths 67 (bottom right); Brian Holloway 54; courtesy Jeanette James 29 (right); Keith Johnson 2–3; Roger Jones 83; courtesy Ben Marshall 63; Dominic Mc Cormack 80–81; Mike Peters 46 (both), 47, 64, 67 (top right), 68, 69, 70–71 (background), 71 (inset), 72–73 (background), 73 (top inset), 77; Richmond upon Thames Council 17 (bottom); Richmond upon Thames Libraries 12 (both), 26; courtesy Brian Rutland 49; Jochen Schwarmann 36, 42 (top); courtesy Emile Snapper 32, 34 (all), 48; Dan van der Vat 89 (artwork by Tricia Cook), 107; Michele Whitby 1, 4, 6, 13, 20, 21, 22, 25, 27, 60 (both), 66, 90–91, 92, 95, 98, 99, 104–105 (all), 108, 109, 110

Index

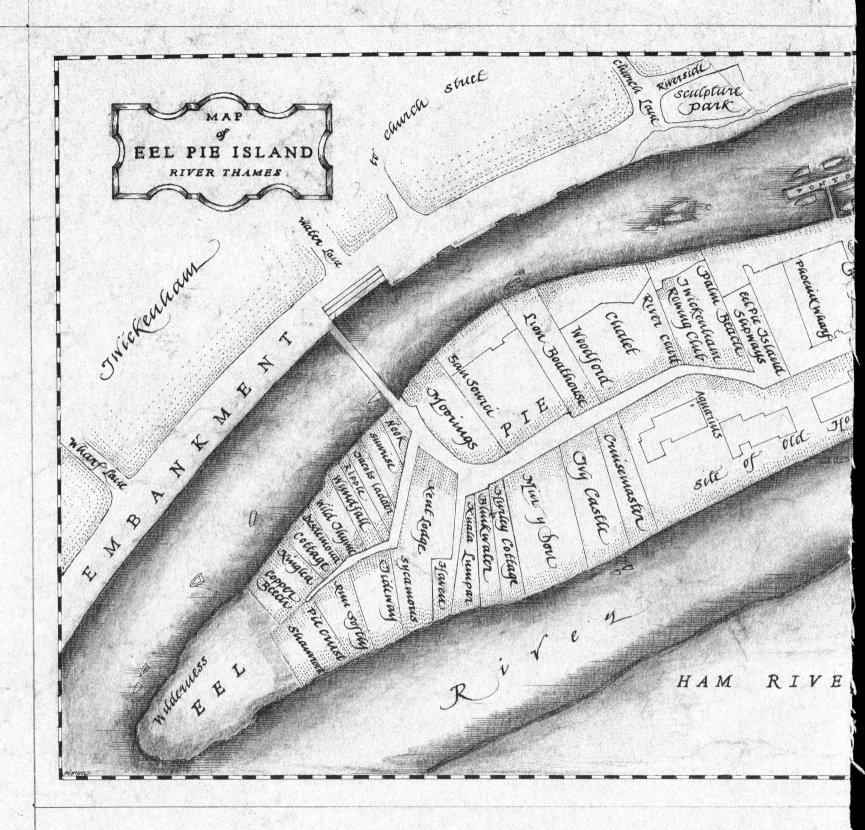